ANIMAL Perplexors

DEDUCTIVE LOGIC PUZZLES

C0-BKE-203

MindWare®

brainy toys for kids of all ages®

www.mindware.com

MindWare® Original Brain Teaser Books

Master math facts, improve deductive reasoning skills, expand vocabularies and more with MindWare's entire line of brain building, boredom busting puzzles. Visit www.mindware.com to see our full selection for all ability levels.

| Logic |

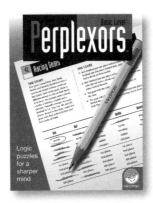

Perplexors: Deductive reasoning and logical elimination are needed to solve these entertaining puzzles.

Analogy Challenges: Build a strong foundation for creative thinking with these quick and clever analogy puzzles.

| Puzzles |

Word Winks: Our visual wordplay puzzles take common phrases and turn them into illustrated brain twisters.

Extreme Dot to Dot: Travel the world, discover amazing animals and more when you connect up 1,400 dots per puzzle.

| Math |

Mathfinder: Solve these clever mysteries by completing math equations and finding your way through the Illustrated mazes.

Math Mosaics: From addition to algebra, this engaging series will have kids cracking codes, plotting patterns and mastering math.

ISBN 978-1-63539-048-3
SKU 68357

for other MindWare products visit
www.mindware.com

Intructions

Logic is a way of thinking about things that you do not have to be taught because you already use this kind of thinking many times a day. When you are faced with a number of choices for anything, you use logic to make your choice. When you use logic, you are being a detective. You use clues to help you make logical decisions.

Logic problems are solved through the process of elimination. If you are presented with five possible answer choices and in one way or another four of those choices are eliminated, you know the fifth possibility must be the correct answer. The best way to learn this process is to work through a problem on your own. In the following exercise, you will be presented with a sample puzzle. In each column, all the possible answer choices are listed. Read through the paragraph and then use the clues, to eliminate answer choices by crossing them out. Once you have an answer, circle it and make sure your answer is crossed-out in the other columns in which it appears as no answer is used more than once. In the following sample puzzle, read the paragraph which describes what you are looking for. When you read the clues, use a pencil to cross-out possibilities, understanding that some clues may not be useful until you have more information.

THE FACTS

Avoid being bitten by a bush viper as there is no antidote to its venom which would turn your organs into something resembling strawberry jelly. The good news is that if you don't climb to the tops of trees in the tropical jungles of the Congo, Uganda, or Kenya, you will never meet a bush viper. The bush viper grows to between 18 to 24 inches, will be either green, olive, or brown, and eats either rodents, birds, or lizards. Bess, Bertha, and Billy were three bush vipers who lived in different countries, were different lengths, and were different colors. Based on the clues, solve the puzzle.

Bess	Bertha	Billy
Congo	Congo	Congo
Uganda	Uganda	Uganda
Kenya	Kenya	Kenya
24 in	24 in	24 in
22 in	22 in	22 in
20 in	20 in	20 in
Green	Green	Green
Olive	Olive	Olive
Brown	Brown	Brown

THE CLUES

1. The smallest viper was olive-colored and lived in Kenya.
2. Billy was bigger than Bertha and Bess wasn't from the Congo where the biggest viper lived.
3. Bertha was smaller than Bess and Bess, by the way, wasn't brown.

Cross out choices as they are eliminated by the clues and circle the choice that is the only choice left. If you you need help, refer to the complete explanation below.

Bess	Bertha	Billy
~~Congo~~	~~Congo~~	(Congo)
(Uganda)	~~Uganda~~	~~Uganda~~
~~Kenya~~	(Kenya)	~~Kenya~~
~~24 in~~	~~24 in~~	(24 in)
(22 in)	~~22 in~~	~~22 in~~
~~20 in~~	(20 in)	~~20 in~~
(Green)	~~Green~~	~~Green~~
~~Olive~~	(Olive)	~~Olive~~
~~Brown~~	~~Brown~~	(Brown)

THE BUSH VIPER SOLUTION

CLUE #1 has useful information that will be used later.

CLUE #2 tells you that since Billy is bigger than Bertha, then Billy isn't 20 inches, olive-colored, or from Kenya. Therefore, all three should be crossed out under Billy. In addition, clue #2 shows that you can also cross out Congo and 24 inches under Bess and Bertha. This leaves Congo and 24 inches as the only possible answers under Billy so those answers should be circled and Uganda and 22 inches should be crossed out.

CLUE #3 allows you to cross out 20 inches under Bess revealing Bertha as the smallest viper living in Kenya and olive-colored (Clue #1). It also tells you that Bess wasn't brown so you can cross out brown under Bess revealing the fact that Bess is green and, therefore, Billy must be brown. The puzzle is now solved!

Tarsier

THE FACTS

Tarsiers are small primates who are now found only on islands in Southeast Asia. Tarsiers have enormous eyes 16mm in diameter and each eyeball is as large as its entire brain. As well as its excellent eyesight, the tarsier has exceptional hearing and equally remarkable jumping ability. It gets this jumping ability from its long hind legs and elongated feet or tarsus bones which give this primate its name. When you add the tarsier's head and body of about 15 centimeters to its hind legs and feet of about 30 centimeters and a 25 centimeter tail you get a total length of 70 centimeters. The tarsier is the only entirely carnivorous primate on the planet and subsists on a diet of Insects, birds, snakes, lizards, and bats. Predators of tarsiers include cats, snakes, and various birds of prey. The tarsier has a lifespan of up to 20 years in the wild. Tammy, Tom, Tillie, Terry, and Tess were 5 tarsiers living on different islands who were different total lengths, had different favorite foods, and were different ages. Based on the clues, solve the puzzle.

Tammy	Tom	Tillie	Terry	Tess
Borneo	Borneo	Borneo	Borneo	Borneo
Sumatra	Sumatra	Sumatra	Sumatra	Sumatra
Luzon	Luzon	Luzon	Luzon	Luzon
Sarawak	Sarawak	Sarawak	Sarawak	Sarawak
Solanesi	Solanesi	Solanesi	Solanesi	Solanesi
70 cm	70 cm	70 cm	70 cm	70 cm
68 cm	68 cm	68 cm	68 cm	68 cm
67 cm	67 cm	67 cm	67 cm	67 cm
65 cm	65 cm	65 cm	65 cm	65 cm
63 cm	63 cm	63 cm	63 cm	63 cm
Insects	Insects	Insects	Insects	Insects
Birds	Birds	Birds	Birds	Birds
Snakes	Snakes	Snakes	Snakes	Snakes
Lizards	Lizards	Lizards	Lizards	Lizards
Bats	Bats	Bats	Bats	Bats
18 Years	18 Years	18 Years	18 Years	18 Years
17 Years	17 Years	17 Years	17 Years	17 Years
16 Years	16 Years	16 Years	16 Years	16 Years
14 Years	14 Years	14 Years	14 Years	14 Years
12 Years	12 Years	12 Years	12 Years	12 Years

THE CLUES

1. The longest tarsier was from Sumatra, liked insects to eat, and was 17 years old.
2. The shortest tarsier was from Luzon, liked birds to eat, and was 16 years old.
3. The oldest tarsier was from Sarawak, liked a bat dinner more than any other food, and was 67 centimeters long.
4. Tillie and Terry lived on the islands of Borneo and Solanesi but who lived on one and who lived on the other, I can't say.
5. Tess was 2 centimeters longer than Terry and Tom was 2 centimeters longer than Tillie and Terry was 2 centimeters longer than Tammy.
6. The youngest tarsier did not live on Solanesi, liked to eat snakes, and was longer than Terry.

THE FACTS

The wild turkey is a large bird native to the forests of North America. Close relatives of the turkey include pheasants, partridges, and grouse. You can tell the state of mind of a male turkey by looking at his head because if his head is blue he is excited and if it turns red he is getting ready to fight. Turkeys weigh between 11 to 24 pounds, are 39 to 49 inches long, and have a wingspan of 4 to 5 feet. Wild turkeys are agile flyers although they seldom fly more than a ¼ of a mile. Wild turkeys are extremely vocal and can be heard to gobble, cluck, putt, purr, yelp, whine, cackle, and kee-kee. Males will gobble, drum, boom, spit, and strut to attract as many females as he can. Hens will lay between 10 to 14 eggs. Newly born chicks are quite mature for their age and can leave the nest within 24 hours to feed themselves. However, there are many predators of both the eggs and the young turkey chicks including raccoons, opossums, skunks, foxes, groundhogs, snakes, owls, coyotes, and hawks. Tara, Toots, Trina, Taylor, and Toni were 5 female turkeys who were different lengths and weights who laid a different number of eggs-that were eaten by a different predator. Based on the clues, solve the puzzle.

Tara	Toots	Trina	Taylor	Toni
49 in	49 in	49 in	49 in	49 in
48 in	48 in	48 in	48 in	48 in
46 in	46 in	46 in	46 in	46 in
44 in	44 in	44 in	44 in	44 in
42 in	42 in	42 in	42 in	42 in
24 lbs	24 lbs	24 lbs	24 lbs	24 lbs
23 lbs	23 lbs	23 lbs	23 lbs	23 lbs
22 lbs	22 lbs	22 lbs	22 lbs	22 lbs
20 lbs	20 lbs	20 lbs	20 lbs	20 lbs
18 lbs	18 lbs	18 lbs	18 lbs	18 lbs
14 Eggs	14 Eggs	14 Eggs	14 Eggs	14 Eggs
13 Eggs	13 Eggs	13 Eggs	13 Eggs	13 Eggs
12 Eggs	12 Eggs	12 Eggs	12 Eggs	12 Eggs
11 Eggs	11 Eggs	11 Eggs	11 Eggs	11 Eggs
10 Eggs	10 Eggs	10 Eggs	10 Eggs	10 Eggs
Raccoon	Raccoon	Raccoon	Raccoon	Raccoon
Skunk	Skunk	Skunk	Skunk	Skunk
Fox	Fox	Fox	Fox	Fox
Groundhog	Groundhog	Groundhog	Groundhog	Groundhog
Coyote	Coyote	Coyote	Coyote	Coyote

THE CLUES

1. The longest turkey laid the most eggs that were eaten by a raccoon but she weighed the least.
2. The 2nd longest turkey laid the 2nd largest number of eggs that were eaten by a coyote but she only weighed 20 pounds.
3. The 3rd longest turkey laid the 3rd largest number of eggs that were eaten by a groundhog and she weighed 22 pounds.
4. The 4th longest turkey laid the 4th largest number of eggs that were eaten by a fox and she weighed 23 pounds.
5. Toots weighed 1 pound more than Tara, and Tara weighed 1 pound more than Toni.
6. Taylor did not lose her eggs to a hungry raccoon.

Canada Goose

THE FACTS

The Canada goose is easily the most recognizable of all the wild goose species with its black head and neck with white patches on its face. It is native to the Arctic and temperate zones of North America but it has been introduced to countries around the world. In the not too distant past, the only sight most people saw of this goose was large v-shaped flights of them as they flew south from the Arctic to escape the winter season. Canada geese subsist on a diet of grass, wheat, rice, corn, beans, seaweed, insects and fish. The Canada goose is usually between 30 to 40 inches long, weighs 6 to 15 pounds, and has a wingspan of 50 to 73 inches. At the age of two, Canada geese pick a mate which they will stay loyal to for the rest of their lives. During mating season, the female will lay between 2 to 9 eggs and both mates will protect the nest. Newly born goslings are able to walk, swim, and find their own food almost as soon as they are born and grow very rapidly. Canada geese have a long lifespan and can live up to 24 years even in the wild. Giles, Grace, Gavin, Gina, and Gary were 5 Canada geese from 5 different countries who were different weights, had different wingspans, and were different ages. Based on the clues, solve the puzzle.

Giles	Grace	Gavin	Gina	Gary
France	France	France	France	France
Germany	Germany	Germany	Germany	Germany
Russia	Russia	Russia	Russia	Russia
China	China	China	China	China
Japan	Japan	Japan	Japan	Japan
16 lbs	16 lbs	16 lbs	16 lbs	16 lbs
15 lbs	15 lbs	15 lbs	15 lbs	15 lbs
13 lbs	13 lbs	13 lbs	13 lbs	13 lbs
12 lbs	12 lbs	12 lbs	12 lbs	12 lbs
11 lbs	11 lbs	11 lbs	11 lbs	11 lbs
73 in wing	73 in wing	73 in wing	73 in wing	73 in wing
71 in wing	71 in wing	71 in wing	71 in wing	71 in wing
70 in wing	70 in wing	70 in wing	70 in wing	70 in wing
68 in wing	68 in wing	68 in wing	68 in wing	68 in wing
66 in wing	66 in wing	66 in wing	66 in wing	66 in wing
20 yrs	20 yrs	20 yrs	20 yrs	20 yrs
18 yrs	18 yrs	18 yrs	18 yrs	18 yrs
16 yrs	16 yrs	16 yrs	16 yrs	16 yrs
15 yrs	15 yrs	15 yrs	15 yrs	15 yrs
13 yrs	13 yrs	13 yrs	13 yrs	13 yrs

THE CLUES

1. The geese from France, Germany, and Russia all had matching weight and age numbers.
2. The oldest goose wasn't from Japan and had the smallest wingspan and weighed the least.
3. Giles, Gina, and Gary did not live in either China or Japan, Gavin was 2 years older than Gina who wasn't from France and the goose from Russia was the youngest goose.
4. Giles had a wingspan 2 inches wider than Gina's wingspan but Gavin had a wingspan 2 inches wider than Grace's wingspan.
5. The youngest goose had the widest wingspan.

House Sparrow

THE FACTS

The house sparrow is the most widely distributed wild bird in the world. It is a small bird no bigger than 18 centimeters long from head to tail with a weight usually between 24 to 50 grams or about 1 ½ ounces. As a species, the house sparrow originated in Europe but because it has an affinity for humans, it gradually spread around the world wherever humans gather. The sparrow is an opportunistic feeder who will eat seeds of weeds as well as cultivated crops such as oats, wheat, cherries, and grapes as well as insects and larvae of all kinds. The sparrow is a very social bird who enjoys the company of other sparrows and they will roost and even nest together and raise their young together. Predators of sparrows include cats and all kinds of hawks but humans take their bite out of the sparrow population as sparrows are a popular food item in some parts of the world. Surviving all that, sparrows have a lifespan of up to 26 years. Sidney, Sylvia, Sheba, Shep, and Shari were 5 sparrows from 5 countries who were different lengths and ages, and had different favorite foods. Based on the clues, solve the puzzle.

Sidney	Sylvia	Sheba	Shep	Shari
France	France	France	France	France
Spain	Spain	Spain	Spain	Spain
Canada	Canada	Canada	Canada	Canada
China	China	China	China	China
Japan	Japan	Japan	Japan	Japan
18 cm	18 cm	18 cm	18 cm	18 cm
17 cm	17 cm	17 cm	17 cm	17 cm
16 cm	16 cm	16 cm	16 cm	16 cm
15 cm	15 cm	15 cm	15 cm	15 cm
14 cm	14 cm	14 cm	14 cm	14 cm
18 Years	18 Years	18 Years	18 Years	18 Years
17 Years	17 Years	17 Years	17 Years	17 Years
16 Years	16 Years	16 Years	16 Years	16 Years
15 Years	15 Years	15 Years	15 Years	15 Years
14 Years	14 Years	14 Years	14 Years	14 Years
Oats	Oats	Oats	Oats	Oats
Wheat	Wheat	Wheat	Wheat	Wheat
Cherries	Cherries	Cherries	Cherries	Cherries
Grapes	Grapes	Grapes	Grapes	Grapes
Insects	Insects	Insects	Insects	Insects

THE CLUES

1. The longest sparrow was the youngest, lived in China, and loved cherries.
2. The 2nd longest sparrow was the 2nd youngest, lived in France, and loved grapes.
3. The 4th longest sparrow was the 2nd oldest, lived in Japan, and loved insects.
4. The shortest sparrow was the oldest, lived in Canada, and loved wheat.
5. Shep was the only sparrow with matching length and age numbers.
6. Sheba was 1 year younger than Shep, Sylvia was 1 centimeter longer than Sheba, and Sidney was older than Shari.

THE FACTS

The binturong is also known as the bearcat and, under that name, is a popular mascot for college teams as the "fighting bearcats." Another popular name for the binturong is the "bear weasel" and this name does a good job of describing this mammal who does look something like a combination of both animals. The binturong marks it territory with scent glands that smell something like popcorn or corn chips. The binturong is fairly large with a head and body length of 28 to 33 inches and a tail of another 26 to 27 inches. They can weigh up to 71 pounds with the females usually weighing about 20% more than the males. The binturong is native to Asian countries with dense forests. Despite being arboreal, the binturong does not leap from tree to tree but prefers to carefully climb down from one tree and carefully climb another all the while keeping its prehensile tail at the ready as an additional gripping tool. The binturong is omnivorous and will eat insects, rats, mice, birds, worms, fish, and fruit. The binturong has a lifespan of up to 25 years. Ben, Binnie, Belle, Brad, and Barry were 5 binturongs from different countries, who were different total lengths, were different weights, and were different ages. Based on the clues, solve the puzzle.

Ben	Binnie	Belle	Brad	Barry
Thailand	Thailand	Thailand	Thailand	Thailand
Vietnam	Vietnam	Vietnam	Vietnam	Vietnam
Laos	Laos	Laos	Laos	Laos
India	India	India	India	India
Indonesia	Indonesia	Indonesia	Indonesia	Indonesia
60 in	60 in	60 in	60 in	60 in
58 in	58 in	58 in	58 in	58 in
55 in	55 in	55 in	55 in	55 in
53 in	53 in	53 in	53 in	53 in
50 in	50 in	50 in	50 in	50 in
70 lbs	70 lbs	70 lbs	70 lbs	70 lbs
65 lbs	65 lbs	65 lbs	65 lbs	65 lbs
60 lbs	60 lbs	60 lbs	60 lbs	60 lbs
55 lbs	55 lbs	55 lbs	55 lbs	55 lbs
50 lbs	50 lbs	50 lbs	50 lbs	50 lbs
20 Years	20 Years	20 Years	20 Years	20 Years
18 Years	18 Years	18 Years	18 Years	18 Years
17 Years	17 Years	17 Years	17 Years	17 Years
16 Years	16 Years	16 Years	16 Years	16 Years
15 Years	15 Years	15 Years	15 Years	15 Years

THE CLUES

1. The binturongs from Thailand, Vietnam, and Laos all had matching length and weight numbers and, in addition, the youngest of those 3 was 2 years older than the youngest binturong of all 5 listed.

2. Binnie was 2 inches less than Belle, Ben was 2 inches less than Brad, and Brad was 5 pounds heavier than Barry.

3. Ben weighed 5 pounds less than the binturong from India but Ben weighed 5 pounds more than the binturong from Thailand who was 1 year older than Binnie.

4. Brad was younger than the binturong from Laos.

Northern Caiman Lizard

THE FACTS

The caiman lizard lives in swampy areas of Brazil, Colombia, Ecuador, Peru, and Guyana. The caiman lizard is the largest lizard in South America with a length of up to 48 inches and a weight of up to 160 ounces. The caiman lizard has short but powerful legs with a large head containing powerful jaws that are usually colored either red or orange. Their diet includes snails, crawfish, clams, fish, rodents, and any kind of insect available. When they eat anything with a hard shell they slide it to the back of their mouths where they crush it with their back teeth and spit out the shells while swallowing the good stuff. The caiman lizard spends most of its time in the water is a good climber and can often be seen relaxing on a tree branch overhanging the water. The caiman lizard enjoys a solitary lifestyle except at mating time. Females will lay 6 to 10 eggs in a hole on a riverbank and will try to disguise the nest. After that, newly born caiman lizards must make it on their own. Caiman lizards who survive can expect a long life of up to 30 years. Five caiman lizards named Carrie, Cathy, Carl, Conrad, and Cindi lived in different countries, had different favorite foods, and were different lengths and ages. Based on the clues, solve the puzzle.

Carrie	Cathy	Carl	Conrad	Cindi
Brazil	Brazil	Brazil	Brazil	Brazil
Columbia	Columbia	Columbia	Columbia	Columbia
Ecuador	Ecuador	Ecuador	Ecuador	Ecuador
Peru	Peru	Peru	Peru	Peru
Guyana	Guyana	Guyana	Guyana	Guyana
Insects	Insects	Insects	Insects	Insects
Snails	Snails	Snails	Snails	Snails
Crawfish	Crawfish	Crawfish	Crawfish	Crawfish
Clams	Clams	Clams	Clams	Clams
Rodents	Rodents	Rodents	Rodents	Rodents
48 in	48 in	48 in	48 in	48 in
47 in	47 in	47 in	47 in	47 in
46 in	46 in	46 in	46 in	46 in
44 in	44 in	44 in	44 in	44 in
42 in	42 in	42 in	42 in	42 in
20 Years	20 Years	20 Years	20 Years	20 Years
18 Years	18 Years	18 Years	18 Years	18 Years
16 Years	16 Years	16 Years	16 Years	16 Years
14 Years	14 Years	14 Years	14 Years	14 Years
10 Years	10 Years	10 Years	10 Years	10 Years

THE CLUES

1. The oldest caiman lizard was from Brazil, loved crawfish, and was 44 inches long.
2. The youngest caiman lizard was from Columbia, loved clams, and was 46 inches long.
3. Carrie and Carl weren't from Ecuador, and they were the two longest lizards with the longest being from Peru.
4. Cathy was 2 years younger than Conrad and Carrie was 2 inches longer than Cindi.
5. Carl is 2 years younger than the insect loving caiman lizard from Peru and Cathy never ate rodents.

THE FACTS

The clown fish is small, being between 10 to 18 centimeters long, which is about 4 to 7 inches. It is a brightly colored fish and may be yellow, orange, or red with white bars or patches. What makes the clown fish unusual is the special relationship it has with the poisonous sea anemones who are mainly composed of toxic chemicals capable of killing any small fish that happens along. However, the clown fish and the sea anemones have formed something called a symbiotic mutualism where they both tolerate each other because they both gain from the relationship in a win-win scenario. When threatened, the clown fish dives into the poisonous tentacles of the sea anemones for protection. In return, the sea anemone gets nutrition from the fecal discharge of the clown fish. Clown fish caught in the open away from a sea anemone will be eaten by just about any larger fish in the water. The lifespan of a clown fish is about 60 months. Five female clown fish named Cora, Callie, Candy, Cyndy, and Chandra who escaped from 5 different sharks, were different lengths, laid a different number of eggs and were different ages. Based on the clues, solve the puzzle.

Cora	Callie	Candy	Cyndy	Chandra
Mako	Mako	Mako	Mako	Mako
Tiger	Tiger	Tiger	Tiger	Tiger
Nurse	Nurse	Nurse	Nurse	Nurse
Blue	Blue	Blue	Blue	Blue
White	White	White	White	White
18 cm	18 cm	18 cm	18 cm	18 cm
17 cm	17 cm	17 cm	17 cm	17 cm
16 cm	16 cm	16 cm	16 cm	16 cm
15 cm	15 cm	15 cm	15 cm	15 cm
14 cm	14 cm	14 cm	14 cm	14 cm
1400 Eggs	1400 Eggs	1400 Eggs	1400 Eggs	1400 Eggs
1300 Eggs	1300 Eggs	1300 Eggs	1300 Eggs	1300 Eggs
1200 Eggs	1200 Eggs	1200 Eggs	1200 Eggs	1200 Eggs
700 Eggs	700 Eggs	700 Eggs	700 Eggs	700 Eggs
600 Eggs	600 Eggs	600 Eggs	600 Eggs	600 Eggs
50 Months	50 Months	50 Months	50 Months	50 Months
48 Months	48 Months	48 Months	48 Months	48 Months
45 Months	45 Months	45 Months	45 Months	45 Months
43 Months	43 Months	43 Months	43 Months	43 Months
41 Months	41 Months	41 Months	41 Months	41 Months

THE CLUES

1. The oldest clown fish barely escaped from a tiger shark, was the longest, and laid the most eggs.
2. The 2nd oldest clown fish barely escaped from a mako shark, was 16 centimeters long, and she laid the 2nd largest number of eggs.
3. The 3rd oldest clown fish barely escaped from a nurse shark, was 17 centimeters long, and she laid the 3rd largest number of eggs.
4. Cora laid ½ as many eggs as Cyndy but Callie laid half as many eggs as Candy.
5. Chandra is 1 centimeter smaller than Candy.
6. Although the youngest clown fish laid the fewest eggs, she wasn't the smallest clown fish and she wasn't chased by a white shark.

Donkey

THE FACTS

The donkey is a domesticated member of the horse family although smaller than the average horse. Today, there are some 41 million donkeys in the world. China has the most donkeys with some 11 million followed by Pakistan, Ethiopia, Mexico, Egypt, India, and Kenya so the donkey is still a valued work partner. Depending on breed, donkeys may be between 31 to 63 inches high at the shoulder and weigh between 200 to as much as 1000 pounds. Donkeys receiving decent treatment and a good diet can expect to live up to 50 years. A somewhat unusual quality of the donkey is its willingness to mate with other members of the horse family. The most common such breeding is between a male donkey and a female horse producing an offspring called a mule. A less common breeding between a male horse and a female donkey produces an offspring known as a "hinny." Donkeys and zebras have mated and produced offspring known as a "zonkie." Some donkeys are raised for their meat and the countries of Italy and China in particular consider donkey flesh a tasty delicacy. The Chinese also value donkey hides for their use in traditional Chinese medicine. Dana, Dave, Dina, Don, and Danny were 5 donkeys from 5 countries who were different heights, weights, and ages. Based on the clues, solve the puzzle.

Dana	Dave	Dina	Don	Danny
China	China	China	China	China
Pakistan	Pakistan	Pakistan	Pakistan	Pakistan
Ethiopia	Ethiopia	Ethiopia	Ethiopia	Ethiopia
Mexico	Mexico	Mexico	Mexico	Mexico
Egypt	Egypt	Egypt	Egypt	Egypt
60 in tall	60 in tall	60 in tall	60 in tall	60 in tall
58 in tall	58 in tall	58 in tall	58 in tall	58 in tall
55 in tall	55 in tall	55 in tall	55 in tall	55 in tall
53 in tall	53 in tall	53 in tall	53 in tall	53 in tall
50 in tall	50 in tall	50 in tall	50 in tall	50 in tall
800 lbs	800 lbs	800 lbs	800 lbs	800 lbs
775 lbs	775 lbs	775 lbs	775 lbs	775 lbs
750 lbs	750 lbs	750 lbs	750 lbs	750 lbs
725 lbs	725 lbs	725 lbs	725 lbs	725 lbs
700 lbs	700 lbs	700 lbs	700 lbs	700 lbs
30 Years	30 Years	30 Years	30 Years	30 Years
25 Years	25 Years	25 Years	25 Years	25 Years
20 Years	20 Years	20 Years	20 Years	20 Years
15 Years	15 Years	15 Years	15 Years	15 Years
10 Years	10 Years	10 Years	10 Years	10 Years

THE CLUES

1. The tallest, heaviest, and oldest donkey was from Ethiopia and the shortest, lightest, and 25-year old donkey was from Mexico.
2. The 20-year old donkey from Egypt weighed 725 pounds and was 53 inches tall.
3. Don was ½ as old as Dana but Danny was ½ as old as Dina.
4. Don wasn't from Pakistan and Don was 2 inches taller than Dina.
5. Danny weighed less than Don.

THE FACTS

There are 7 species of gar in the world including the alligator gar which can grow up to 10 feet and weigh 300 pounds or so. While not growing that large, other species of gar are still quite large and grow up to 36 inches and weigh 60 pounds or so. Gar have long armored bodies with long jaws filled with long sharp teeth but this fearsome weaponry is not what has enabled the gar to survive over so many million years. Gar come equipped with swim bladders which also serve as lungs should the need arise. Gar have the ability to survive in low oxygen water that would kill other fish by simply going to the surface and using its "lung" to breathe air. Gar hunt by waiting for prey to come along and then striking quickly with a sideward lunge. Gar will eat any smaller fish such as perch, bluegills, sunfish, and herring as well as crawfish, frogs, and even turtles. Gar have a lifespan of 50 years for females while male gar only live for about 30 years. Gayle, Gordy, Gene, Gigi, and Gwen were 5 gar who had different favorite foods, and were different lengths, weights, and ages. Based on the clues, solve the puzzle.

Gayle	Gordy	Gene	Gigi	Gwen
Perch	Perch	Perch	Perch	Perch
Bluegill	Bluegill	Bluegill	Bluegill	Bluegill
Herring	Herring	Herring	Herring	Herring
Frog	Frog	Frog	Frog	Frog
Crawfish	Crawfish	Crawfish	Crawfish	Crawfish
36 in	36 in	36 in	36 in	36 in
34 in	34 in	34 in	34 in	34 in
32 in	32 in	32 in	32 in	32 in
31 in	31 in	31 in	31 in	31 in
29 in	29 in	29 in	29 in	29 in
50 lbs	50 lbs	50 lbs	50 lbs	50 lbs
49 lbs	49 lbs	49 lbs	49 lbs	49 lbs
47 lbs	47 lbs	47 lbs	47 lbs	47 lbs
46 lbs	46 lbs	46 lbs	46 lbs	46 lbs
43 lbs	43 lbs	43 lbs	43 lbs	43 lbs
20 Years	20 Years	20 Years	20 Years	20 Years
19 Years	19 Years	19 Years	19 Years	19 Years
18 Years	18 Years	18 Years	18 Years	18 Years
17 Years	17 Years	17 Years	17 Years	17 Years
16 Years	16 Years	16 Years	16 Years	16 Years

THE CLUES

1. The age numbers of the 3 youngest gar are exactly ½ the size of their size in inches number.
2. The youngest gar weighs the least, the next youngest weighs 46 pounds, the next youngest weighs 47 pounds on up to the oldest gar who is the heaviest.
3. Gayle and Gordy's favorite food was not perch, bluegills, or herring and the youngest gar's favorite food was perch.
4. Gigi was 2 years older than Gordy and Gigi weighed 1 pound more than Gwen.
5. The longest gar loved crunchy crawfish and the shortest gar loved bluegills.
6. Gayle was 1 year older than Gene and Gwen was longer than Gigi.

Hercules Beetle

THE FACTS

The Hercules beetle is one of the largest species of beetle in the world and is most famous for its strength. For its size, it is considered the strongest creature on the planet capable of lifting an object weighing up to 272 ounces or about 17 pounds. This is the equivalent of a normal human being lifting a good sized truck. The Hercules beetle can reach lengths of up to 20 centimeters and the males grow pincers out of their foreheads that can grow as long as their bodies. This beetle is omnivorous and it mainly subsists on decaying vegetable matter including leaves, berries, fruit, wood, and insects. Life begins for a Hercules beetle after a female lays up to 100 eggs usually on the jungle floor. The beetle then moves into a larval stage where it remains for up to 24 months tunneling underground searching for food. As larvae, the beetle grows quite large and, in size, looks something like a Twinkie. The sole reason the Hercules beetle becomes an adult is to reproduce and after a short life of only about 4 months it dies. Hester, Helga, Heidi, Helen, and Hilda were 5 Hercules beetles who lived in different countries, were different lengths, lifted different weights, and laid different numbers of eggs. Based on the clues, solve the puzzle.

Hester	Helga	Heidi	Helen	Hilda
Brazil	Brazil	Brazil	Brazil	Brazil
Peru	Peru	Peru	Peru	Peru
Mexico	Mexico	Mexico	Mexico	Mexico
Columbia	Columbia	Columbia	Columbia	Columbia
Ecuador	Ecuador	Ecuador	Ecuador	Ecuador
20 cm	20 cm	20 cm	20 cm	20 cm
19 cm	19 cm	19 cm	19 cm	19 cm
18 cm	18 cm	18 cm	18 cm	18 cm
17 cm	17 cm	17 cm	17 cm	17 cm
16 cm	16 cm	16 cm	16 cm	16 cm
270 oz	270 oz	270 oz	270 oz	270 oz
268 oz	268 oz	268 oz	268 oz	268 oz
265 oz	265 oz	265 oz	265 oz	265 oz
263 oz	263 oz	263 oz	263 oz	263 oz
260 oz	260 oz	260 oz	260 oz	260 oz
100 Eggs	100 Eggs	100 Eggs	100 Eggs	100 Eggs
95 Eggs	95 Eggs	95 Eggs	95 Eggs	95 Eggs
90 Eggs	90 Eggs	90 Eggs	90 Eggs	90 Eggs
85 Eggs	85 Eggs	85 Eggs	85 Eggs	85 Eggs
80 Eggs	80 Eggs	80 Eggs	80 Eggs	80 Eggs

THE CLUES

1. The longest beetle was from Ecuador, lifted 260 ounces and laid the fewest eggs.
2. The 2nd longest beetle was from Brazil, lifted 270 ounces, and laid the most eggs.
3. Helen and Hilda were from Peru and Mexico but maybe not in that exact order.
4. Hester was 1 centimeter longer than Hilda and Helga was 1 centimeter longer than Heidi.
5. The shortest beetle was from Peru, lifted 268 ounces and laid 95 eggs. Hester lifted 3 ounces less than Helen.
6. The beetle from Columbia laid more eggs than the beetle from Mexico.

Iriomote Cat

THE FACTS

The Iriomote cat is a subspecies of the leopard cat which is relatively common throughout South and East Asia. The leopard cat is a small wild cat about the size of a good-sized domestic cat. Mystery surrounds the reason how the leopard cat managed to populate the 110 square mile island of Iriomote located in the ocean near the island nation of Japan. The answer was supplied by geologists who said Iriomote was connected to the mainland of Asia by a land bridge some 240 thousand years ago. The Iriomote cat didn't just survive, it managed to remain undiscovered until 1962. Iriomote cats grow to about 60 centimeters or about 24 inches and weigh up to 176 ounces or roughly 11 pounds. The Iriomote cat eats birds, reptiles, bats, flying foxes, skinks, frogs, ducks, and anything else it may find. The Iriomote cat is unusual when it eats birds because unlike other cats it will not remove the feathers and instead will swallow the bird whole, feathers and all. These cats live solitary lives and will only come together when it is time to breed. The lifespan of the Iriomote cat is about 9 years. Inez, Igor, Iggy, Ilsa, and Irene were 5 Iriomote cats who were different lengths, weights, had different favorite foods, and were different ages. Based on the clues, solve the puzzle.

Inez	Igor	Iggy	Ilsa	Irene
60 cm	60 cm	60 cm	60 cm	60 cm
59 cm	59 cm	59 cm	59 cm	59 cm
58 cm	58 cm	58 cm	58 cm	58 cm
56 cm	56 cm	56 cm	56 cm	56 cm
54 cm	54 cm	54 cm	54 cm	54 cm
176 oz	176 oz	176 oz	176 oz	176 oz
172 oz	172 oz	172 oz	172 oz	172 oz
168 oz	168 oz	168 oz	168 oz	168 oz
166 oz	166 oz	166 oz	166 oz	166 oz
164 oz	164 oz	164 oz	164 oz	164 oz
Rats	Rats	Rats	Rats	Rats
Birds	Birds	Birds	Birds	Birds
Snakes	Snakes	Snakes	Snakes	Snakes
Frogs	Frogs	Frogs	Frogs	Frogs
Bats	Bats	Bats	Bats	Bats
8 Years	8 Years	8 Years	8 Years	8 Years
7 Years	7 Years	7 Years	7 Years	7 Years
6 Years	6 Years	6 Years	6 Years	6 Years
5 Years	5 Years	5 Years	5 Years	5 Years
4 Years	4 Years	4 Years	4 Years	4 Years

THE CLUES

1. The longest cat loved to eat birds, weighed more than 166 oz, and was older than 5 years of age.
2. The shortest cat loved to eat snakes, weighed more than 166 oz, and was 6 years old.
3. The 59 centimeter cat loved to eat rats, weighed more than 166 oz, and was older than 5 years.
4. The youngest cat loved to eat frogs, weighed the least, and was one of the 3 longest cats. The longest was also the oldest cat.
5. Inez didn't like to eat rats, birds, or snakes, Inez weighed more than Igor, and Inez was not one of the 3 longest cats.
6. Ilsa was 1 year older than Inez, Iggy was 1 year older than the rat-loving cat and Ilsa did not eat birds.
7. Igor was 2 centimeters longer than Inez and Irene was not the heaviest cat but she weighed more than Iggy.

Jackal

THE FACTS

The jackal is a relatively small, opportunistic omnivore of the genus "canis" which includes the wolf, dog, coyote, and Australian Dingo. There are 8 species of jackal but all are about the same size being up to 42 inches in length with the tail adding another 10 inches or so. They all are about 20 inches tall at the shoulder and weigh up to 35 pounds. Jackals find one mate and stay together with that mate for life. Jackals are devoted to family and after the female gives birth to 1 to 4 pups, both parents will feed, guard, groom, and play with their young for nearly a year. Surviving childhood, jackals have a normal lifespan of about 12 years in the wild. Although thought of as strictly scavengers living off the leavings of other animals, the jackal is a proficient hunter and will eat mice, rats, birds, small antelope, and even fruit, berries, and grass if it comes to that. Jack, Jill, Josey, Jenny, and Jane were 5 jackals native to different countries and were different lengths, weights, and ages. Based on the clues, solve the puzzle.

Jack	Jill	Josey	Jenny	Jane
Egypt	Egypt	Egypt	Egypt	Egypt
India	India	India	India	India
Congo	Congo	Congo	Congo	Congo
Kenya	Kenya	Kenya	Kenya	Kenya
Rwanda	Rwanda	Rwanda	Rwanda	Rwanda
42 in	42 in	42 in	42 in	42 in
41 in	41 in	41 in	41 in	41 in
40 in	40 in	40 in	40 in	40 in
39 in	39 in	39 in	39 in	39 in
38 in	38 in	38 in	38 in	38 in
35 lbs	35 lbs	35 lbs	35 lbs	35 lbs
34 lbs	34 lbs	34 lbs	34 lbs	34 lbs
33 lbs	33 lbs	33 lbs	33 lbs	33 lbs
32 lbs	32 lbs	32 lbs	32 lbs	32 lbs
31 lbs	31 lbs	31 lbs	31 lbs	31 lbs
10 Years	10 Years	10 Years	10 Years	10 Years
9 Years	9 Years	9 Years	9 Years	9 Years
8 Years	8 Years	8 Years	8 Years	8 Years
7 Years	7 Years	7 Years	7 Years	7 Years
6 Years	6 Years	6 Years	6 Years	6 Years

THE CLUES

1. The 2 youngest jackals were from India and the Congo and the 8 year old jackal was from Egypt.
2. The tallest jackal was the heaviest, the 2nd tallest was the 2nd heaviest, the 3rd tallest was the 3rd heaviest and so on.
3. The youngest jackal was the tallest, the 7 year old was the 2nd heaviest, the 8 year old was the 3rd tallest, and the 9 year old weighed 32 pounds.
4. Jack and Jill were from Kenya and Rwanda and Jane was 1 year younger than Jill.
5. Jenny was not from the Congo, Jill was not from Rwanda, and, of course, Josey was taller than Jenny.

THE FACTS

The leopard seal is native to the waters of the Antarctic. It is the 2nd largest seal with only the elephant seal being larger. The leopard seal is large and muscular with a light gray coat and black spots which gave it its name. Make no mistake about it, the leopard seal like the leopard itself is a deadly predator. Leopard seals are formidable with a length between 8 and 12 feet and a weight of between 450 and 1300 pounds. They seem to specialize and even delight in killing every species of penguin found in the Antarctic. Leopard seals are mostly solitary creatures except at mating time. Male leopard seals attract a mate by hanging upside down while chirping and moaning in a repeated pattern or "song." Larry, Lucy, Linda, Les, and Lulu were 5 leopard seals who killed and ate a different number of 4 species of penguins one recent month. Based on the clues, solve the puzzle.

Larry	Lucy	Linda	Les	Lulu
10 King	10 King	10 King	10 King	10 King
8 King	8 King	8 King	8 King	8 King
6 King	6 King	6 King	6 King	6 King
4 King	4 King	4 King	4 King	4 King
2 King	2 King	2 King	2 King	2 King
5 Adelie	5 Adelie	5 Adelie	5 Adelie	5 Adelie
4 Adelie	4 Adelie	4 Adelie	4 Adelie	4 Adelie
3 Adelie	3 Adelie	3 Adelie	3 Adelie	3 Adelie
2 Adelie	2 Adelie	2 Adelie	2 Adelie	2 Adelie
1 Adelie	1 Adelie	1 Adelie	1 Adelie	1 Adelie
10 Gentoo	10 Gentoo	10 Gentoo	10 Gentoo	10 Gentoo
8 Gentoo	8 Gentoo	8 Gentoo	8 Gentoo	8 Gentoo
6 Gentoo	6 Gentoo	6 Gentoo	6 Gentoo	6 Gentoo
4 Gentoo	4 Gentoo	4 Gentoo	4 Gentoo	4 Gentoo
2 Gentoo	2 Gentoo	2 Gentoo	2 Gentoo	2 Gentoo
5 Emperor	5 Emperor	5 Emperor	5 Emperor	5 Emperor
4 Emperor	4 Emperor	4 Emperor	4 Emperor	4 Emperor
3 Emperor	3 Emperor	3 Emperor	3 Emperor	3 Emperor
2 Emperor	2 Emperor	2 Emperor	2 Emperor	2 Emperor
1 Emperor	1 Emperor	1 Emperor	1 Emperor	1 Emperor

THE CLUES

1. One leopard seal ate the most of all 4 species of penguin while another leopard seal ate the fewest of all 4 species of penguin.

2. Another leopard seal ate the 3rd largest number of all 4 species of penguin while the remaining 2 leopard seals each ate the 2nd largest number of penguins two times.

3. Linda ate twice as many King penguins as Les and Larry ate half as many King penguins as Les, and Les ate twice as many Adelie penguins as Larry.

4. Lucy and Les ate a combined total of 10 king penguins.

Sea Otter

THE FACTS

The sea otter is a marine mammal living in the coastal waters of the northern and eastern Pacific Ocean. The sea otter is closely related to badgers, weasels, martens, ferrets, minks, and wolverines. The sea otter is the largest member of that family but is the smallest of all marine mammals. Sea otters reach an adult weight of between 31 to 99 pounds. Unlike other sea mammals who rely on the layers of fat to insulate themselves from the cold ocean, sea otters rely on a remarkable fur coat which is the densest of any fur anywhere else. Sea otters have a varied diet of sea urchins, snails, fish, clams, crabs, barnacles, mussels, and abalone. Sea otters use rocks as tools to bash open hard-shelled food items. Sea otters are polygamous and will mate with different partners over a lifetime. Female sea otters are devoted mothers and will usually give birth to 1 pup which it will groom and nurture for nearly a full year. Sea otters have a normal lifespan of about 23 years. Ozzie, Ollie, Oppie, Olive, and Oona were 5 sea otters from different locations who had different favorite foods and were different weights and ages. Based on the clues, solve the puzzle.

Ozzie	Ollie	Oppie	Olive	Oona
Russia	Russia	Russia	Russia	Russia
Aleutians	Aleutians	Aleutians	Aleutians	Aleutians
Alaska	Alaska	Alaska	Alaska	Alaska
British Columbia	British Columbia	British Columbia	British Columbia	British Columbia
Washington	Washington	Washington	Washington	Washington
Clams	Clams	Clams	Clams	Clams
Mussels	Mussels	Mussels	Mussels	Mussels
Abalone	Abalone	Abalone	Abalone	Abalone
Sea Urchins	Sea Urchins	Sea Urchins	Sea Urchins	Sea Urchins
Snails	Snails	Snails	Snails	Snails
90 lbs	90 lbs	90 lbs	90 lbs	90 lbs
85 lbs	85 lbs	85 lbs	85 lbs	85 lbs
80 lbs	80 lbs	80 lbs	80 lbs	80 lbs
75 lbs	75 lbs	75 lbs	75 lbs	75 lbs
70 lbs	70 lbs	70 lbs	70 lbs	70 lbs
20 Years	20 Years	20 Years	20 Years	20 Years
18 Years	18 Years	18 Years	18 Years	18 Years
17 Years	17 Years	17 Years	17 Years	17 Years
16 Years	16 Years	16 Years	16 Years	16 Years
14 Years	14 Years	14 Years	14 Years	14 Years

THE CLUES

1. The heaviest sea otter lived in the Aleutians, loved mussels, and was not the oldest or youngest.
2. The lightest sea otter lived in British Columbia, loved sea urchins, and was not the oldest or youngest.
3. The 85 pound sea otter lived in Alaska, loved snails, and was not the oldest or youngest of the five.
4. The youngest sea otter lived in Russia, loved clams, and weighed 75 pounds.
5. Ozzie, Ollie, and Oppie did not live in Russia or Washington.
6. Oona weighed 5 pounds more than Oppie, Ozzie weighed 5 pounds more than Olive, and Oppie was 2 years older than Ozzie.

THE FACTS

The king vulture is the second largest scavenger bird after the condor. It has a bald head and neck which prevents bacteria from the rotting flesh it eats from ruining its feathers. The king vulture has a strong bill with a hooked tip and a sharp cutting edge which allows it to rip open the carcass of animals with the thickest hides. Adult king vultures are 27 to 32 inches long, weigh 6 to 10 pounds, and have a 4 to 6 foot wingspan. When feeding, the king vulture has a rasp-like tongue which allows it to pull the flesh off bones. If a king vulture becomes overheated, it will defecate on its legs to cool off in a process called "vrodidrosis." King vultures mate for life and are devoted parents. King vultures have a normal lifespan of about 30 years. Vicky, Vera, Val, Viola, and Vlad were 5 king vultures who each had a different favorite carcass to eat, lived in a different country, had different wingspans and were different ages. Based on the clues, solve the puzzle.

Vicky	Vera	Val	Viola	Vlad
Cow	Cow	Cow	Cow	Cow
Goat	Goat	Goat	Goat	Goat
Deer	Deer	Deer	Deer	Deer
Horse	Horse	Horse	Horse	Horse
Pig	Pig	Pig	Pig	Pig
Mexico	Mexico	Mexico	Mexico	Mexico
Peru	Peru	Peru	Peru	Peru
Brazil	Brazil	Brazil	Brazil	Brazil
Columbia	Columbia	Columbia	Columbia	Columbia
Panama	Panama	Panama	Panama	Panama
72 in wing	72 in wing	72 in wing	72 in wing	72 in wing
70 in wing	70 in wing	70 in wing	70 in wing	70 in wing
69 in wing	69 in wing	69 in wing	69 in wing	69 in wing
68 in wing	68 in wing	68 in wing	68 in wing	68 in wing
67 in wing	67 in wing	67 in wing	67 in wing	67 in wing
25 Years	25 Years	25 Years	25 Years	25 Years
23 Years	23 Years	23 Years	23 Years	23 Years
20 Years	20 Years	20 Years	20 Years	20 Years
17 Years	17 Years	17 Years	17 Years	17 Years
14 Years	14 Years	14 Years	14 Years	14 Years

THE CLUES

1. The oldest did not have the widest wingspan, the 2nd oldest did not have the 2nd widest wingspan, and the same holds true for the 3rd, 4th, and 5th oldest who didn't have the 3rd, 4th, and 5th widest wingspans.
2. The vulture who loved rotting pig flesh lived in Panama, the goat loving vulture lived in Brazil, and the cow loving vulture lived in Columbia and was the youngest vulture on the list.
3. Vicky and Vera lived in Mexico and Peru, had wingspans wider than 69 inches and had a combined age of 48 years.
4. Viola's wingspan was 1 inch wider than Vlad's wingspan and neither Viola and Vlad liked the taste of rotten pig.
5. Vlad was 3 years younger than Viola, Val was 3 years younger than Vicky, and Vera didn't live in Mexico.
6. The oldest king vulture loved the taste of rotting horse flesh.

THE FACTS

Also known as a vinta ground squirrel, the potgut is a mammal that is often confused with a prairie dog as they prefer somewhat similar habitats. An adult potgut weighs between 285 to 600 grams, is about 25 to 30 centimeters in length with a tail adding another 6 to 8 centimeters. This ground squirrel subsists on a diet of grass, aquatic plants, leaves, seeds, beetles, crickets, grasshoppers, and anything else remotely edible. The potgut spends 9 months a year in a deep sleep so when it emerges from its burrow in early spring it is in a hurry to breed. Females give birth to about 2 to 6 young after only a one-month gestation and the newborn are ready to leave the birthing burrow after only 24 days. They have to be in a hurry as they have to get everything done before they go to bed again for another 9 months. This ground squirrel has many predators including badgers, weasels, hawks, coyotes, and wolves. Surviving all that, the potgut has a normal lifespan of 7 years with about 5 years of that time spent sleeping. Polly, Paula, Penny, Pearl, and Patty were 5 potguts who were different lengths, had given birth to a different number of young, were different ages, and had escaped from a different predator. Based on the clues, solve the puzzle.

Polly	Paula	Penny	Pearl	Patty
38 cm	38 cm	38 cm	38 cm	38 cm
36 cm	36 cm	36 cm	36 cm	36 cm
35 cm	35 cm	35 cm	35 cm	35 cm
34 cm	34 cm	34 cm	34 cm	34 cm
32 cm	32 cm	32 cm	32 cm	32 cm
6 Young	6 Young	6 Young	6 Young	6 Young
5 Young	5 Young	5 Young	5 Young	5 Young
4 Young	4 Young	4 Young	4 Young	4 Young
3 Young	3 Young	3 Young	3 Young	3 Young
2 Young	2 Young	2 Young	2 Young	2 Young
6 Years Old	6 Years Old	6 Years Old	6 Years Old	6 Years Old
5 Years Old	5 Years Old	5 Years Old	5 Years Old	5 Years Old
4 Years Old	4 Years Old	4 Years Old	4 Years Old	4 Years Old
3 Years Old	3 Years Old	3 Years Old	3 Years Old	3 Years Old
2 Years Old	2 Years Old	2 Years Old	2 Years Old	2 Years Old
Badger	Badger	Badger	Badger	Badger
Weasel	Weasel	Weasel	Weasel	Weasel
Hawk	Hawk	Hawk	Hawk	Hawk
Coyote	Coyote	Coyote	Coyote	Coyote
Wolf	Wolf	Wolf	Wolf	Wolf

THE CLUES

1. The oldest potgut was 34 centimeter from head to tail, was nearly killed by a hawk, and gave birth to only 2 young.

2. The 5,4,3, and 2 year old potguts oddly each gave birth to 1 more young than their ages so the 5 year old had 6 young and so on.

3. The coyote nearly caught the youngest potgut and the wolf nearly caught the 3 year old potgut who was only 32 centimeters long.

4. Paula was only 2 centimeters longer than Penny, Penny was 2 centimeters longer than Polly, and Patty was longer than Polly by only 1 centimeter.

5. Penny wasn't chased by a weasel and Paula was 1 year older than Penny.

THE FACTS

The water dragon is an arboreal agamid which is to say it is a tree-dwelling iguana-like lizard. Female adults can reach a length of 24 inches or so from head to tail while males may grow to as much as 36 inches. Water dragons can weigh as much as 40 ounces. When they are not eating a diet of ants, spiders, crickets, beetles, caterpillars, larvae, fish, mice, frogs, tadpoles, and smaller lizards, they like to bask on tree branches overhanging the water. If danger approaches, they can drop into the water and swim away underwater where they can stay for as long as 90 minutes. Males seeking to mate compete with other males by waving their arms at each other with the fastest waving dragon winning the right to reproduce. After mating, the female water dragon will dig a shallow burrow and lay 6 to 18 eggs. Newly hatched water dragons are pretty much on their own. Water dragons can live for as long as 20 years. Walt, Willa, Wallis, Winnie, and Westy were 5 water dragons who were different ages and, one recent day ate a different number of food items. Based on the clues, solve the puzzle.

Walt	Willa	Wallis	Winnie	Westy
16 Years Old	16 Years Old	16 Years Old	16 Years Old	16 Years Old
14 Years Old	14 Years Old	14 Years Old	14 Years Old	14 Years Old
12 Years Old	12 Years Old	12 Years Old	12 Years Old	12 Years Old
8 Years Old	8 Years Old	8 Years Old	8 Years Old	8 Years Old
6 Years Old	6 Years Old	6 Years Old	6 Years Old	6 Years Old
16 Ants	16 Ants	16 Ants	16 Ants	16 Ants
14 Ants	14 Ants	14 Ants	14 Ants	14 Ants
12 Ants	12 Ants	12 Ants	12 Ants	12 Ants
8 Ants	8 Ants	8 Ants	8 Ants	8 Ants
6 Ants	6 Ants	6 Ants	6 Ants	6 Ants
16 Crickets	16 Crickets	16 Crickets	16 Crickets	16 Crickets
14 Crickets	14 Crickets	14 Crickets	14 Crickets	14 Crickets
12 Crickets	12 Crickets	12 Crickets	12 Crickets	12 Crickets
8 Crickets	8 Crickets	8 Crickets	8 Crickets	8 Crickets
6 Crickets	6 Crickets	6 Crickets	6 Crickets	6 Crickets
16 Beetles	16 Beetles	16 Beetles	16 Beetles	16 Beetles
14 Beetles	14 Beetles	14 Beetles	14 Beetles	14 Beetles
12 Beetles	12 Beetles	12 Beetles	12 Beetles	12 Beetles
8 Beetles	8 Beetles	8 Beetles	8 Beetles	8 Beetles
6 Beetles	6 Beetles	6 Beetles	6 Beetles	6 Beetles

THE CLUES

1. Wallis had the highest number in 2 of the 4 categories and Winnie had the highest number in 2 of the 4 categories and neither of them had the lowest number in any category.

2. Willa had the lowest number in 2 of the 4 categories and Westy had the lowest number in 2 of the 4 categories.

3. Willa had the 2nd highest number in 2 of the 4 categories and Westy had the 2nd highest number in 2 of the 4 categories.

4. Walt, who was older than Winnie, ate more beetles than Winnie, and Willa, who was ½ as old as Walt, ate ½ as many ants as Walt.

5. Wallis ate 2 more crickets than Westy.

THE FACTS

The loris is a small nocturnal primate native to Southeast Asia. They have round heads, a narrow protruding snout, and large eyes useful for seeing at night. The loris ranges in length from 7 to 15 inches and their weight ranges from 9 ounces to an unusually heavy 74 ounces. The loris moves slowly and silently and climbs very deliberately with three out of four limbs holding on to the tree at all times. If threatened, the loris will generally stop moving altogether and remain motionless. One thing the loris has going for it that is unique among primates is a toxic bite. The loris is able to manufacture poison by combining the secretions from a gland on their arm with their saliva. This toxin serves as a deterrent to predators but is also useful for when a loris has to leave an infant unattended. The loris parent will cover their infants' fur with their poison spit hoping to ward off predators. The loris is an omnivore and will eat just about anything it can including mice, rats, fruit, tree gum, insects, birds, leaves, eggs, and anything else that comes to hand. The normal lifespan for a loris is about 20 years. Livia, Lane, Layla, Lorna, and Louis were 5 lorises who, in a recent week, ate a different number of food items. Based on the clues, solve the puzzle.

Livia	Lane	Layla	Lorna	Louis
5 Mice	5 Mice	5 Mice	5 Mice	5 Mice
4 Mice	4 Mice	4 Mice	4 Mice	4 Mice
3 Mice	3 Mice	3 Mice	3 Mice	3 Mice
2 Mice	2 Mice	2 Mice	2 Mice	2 Mice
1 Mouse	1 Mouse	1 Mouse	1 Mouse	1 Mouse
50 Insects	50 Insects	50 Insects	50 Insects	50 Insects
48 Insects	48 Insects	48 Insects	48 Insects	48 Insects
45 Insects	45 Insects	45 Insects	45 Insects	45 Insects
40 Insects	40 Insects	40 Insects	40 Insects	40 Insects
35 Insects	35 Insects	35 Insects	35 Insects	35 Insects
25 Leaves	25 Leaves	25 Leaves	25 Leaves	25 Leaves
24 Leaves	24 Leaves	24 Leaves	24 Leaves	24 Leaves
20 Leaves	20 Leaves	20 Leaves	20 Leaves	20 Leaves
15 Leaves	15 Leaves	15 Leaves	15 Leaves	15 Leaves
10 Leaves	10 Leaves	10 Leaves	10 Leaves	10 Leaves
10 Eggs	10 Eggs	10 Eggs	10 Eggs	10 Eggs
8 Eggs	8 Eggs	8 Eggs	8 Eggs	8 Eggs
6 Eggs	6 Eggs	6 Eggs	6 Eggs	6 Eggs
4 Eggs	4 Eggs	4 Eggs	4 Eggs	4 Eggs
2 Eggs	2 Eggs	2 Eggs	2 Eggs	2 Eggs

THE CLUES

1. Except for Layla, each loris in turn ate the most of one food item, the 2nd most of another food item, the 4th most of another food item, and the 5th most of still another item.
2. Lorna ate more Insects than Louis but Louis ate more Insects than Layla.
3. Livia ate more leaves than Lane but Lane ate more leaves than Layla.
4. Lane did not eat the most eggs but Lane ate more eggs than Livia and Louis ate more mice than Lorna.

Potto

THE FACTS

The potto is a nocturnal and arboreal small primate native to the rain forests of tropical Africa. The potto, while widespread, is seldom seen because it very rarely leaves the treetops and spends the day hiding and sleeping. The potto is only about 30 to 39 centimeters in length and weighs between 21 to 56 ounces. For some reason, the potto has no index finger but it does have opposable thumbs and a strong grip useful for an animal who lives in the trees. The potto has an unusual defense against predators as it has a series of unusual growths on its neck. When threatened, the potto will cover its face and butt an aggressor with its neck. Pottos are well equipped for grooming as it has front teeth that look like the teeth on a comb and a special "toilet claw" on its hind legs which is specifically adapted to grooming. Grooming is a very important part of a potto's life as mates are chosen by the grooming ritual. A male and female potto will hang upside down on a high branch and groom each other with their teeth and toilet claws. Pottos have few predators and have a lifespan of about 25 years. Paul, Patrick, Paris, Pete, and Pella were 5 pottos living in different countries, and were different lengths, weights, and ages. Based on the clues, solve the puzzle.

Paul	Patrick	Paris	Pete	Pella
Congo	Congo	Congo	Congo	Congo
Guinea	Guinea	Guinea	Guinea	Guinea
Kenya	Kenya	Kenya	Kenya	Kenya
Uganda	Uganda	Uganda	Uganda	Uganda
Senegal	Senegal	Senegal	Senegal	Senegal
39 cm	39 cm	39 cm	39 cm	39 cm
38 cm	38 cm	38 cm	38 cm	38 cm
36 cm	36 cm	36 cm	36 cm	36 cm
34 cm	34 cm	34 cm	34 cm	34 cm
32 cm	32 cm	32 cm	32 cm	32 cm
56 oz	56 oz	56 oz	56 oz	56 oz
53 oz	53 oz	53 oz	53 oz	53 oz
50 oz	50 oz	50 oz	50 oz	50 oz
48 oz	48 oz	48 oz	48 oz	48 oz
45 oz	45 oz	45 oz	45 oz	45 oz
20 Years	20 Years	20 Years	20 Years	20 Years
18 Years	18 Years	18 Years	18 Years	18 Years
17 Years	17 Years	17 Years	17 Years	17 Years
16 Years	16 Years	16 Years	16 Years	16 Years
14 Years	14 Years	14 Years	14 Years	14 Years

THE CLUES

1. The oldest potto was both the longest and lightest potto of the 5 listed here, the 18 year old was 38 centimeters and 48 ounces, and the 17 year old was 36 centimeters and 50 ounces, and the 16 year old was 34 centimeters and 53 ounces.
2. The 3 oldest pottos lived in Guinea, Uganda, and Senegal and the 3 heaviest pottos lived in Congo, Guinea, and Kenya.
3. Pete was 2 centimeters longer than Pella but Pella weighed 3 ounces more than Pete and Pete was 2 years older than Pella.
4. Paul weighed 3 ounces more than Patrick.
5. The oldest did not live in Uganda and the youngest did not live in Kenya.

THE FACTS

Seeing pictures of frogfish, it is easy to see how they get their name because they resemble brightly colored frogs as they crawl around the ocean floor on fins that look a lot like legs. To add to that effect, frogfish have relatively short, stocky scale-less bodies of between 2 to 15 inches in length. Frogfish may be any color that helps it blend into the color of its surrounding. Typically, a frogfish will sit on the ocean floor until it spots a likely meal. The frogfish will slowly inch along until it gets near enough to strike with blazing speed and swallow its catch whole. Frogfish have the ability to enlarge its jaws and stomach enabling it to eat fish twice its size. Female frogfish swell up with up to 180,000 eggs which signals to the male that she is ready to lay a string of eggs which will float to the surface and hatch. The male must follow the female carefully to fertilize her eggs and scoot away quickly before she eats him. The precise lifespan of frogfish is unknown, but it is estimated to be at least 10 years or more. Frank, Flo, Filene, Farrah, and Foster were 5 frogfish living in different waters who were different colors, lengths, and ages. Based on the clues, solve the puzzle.

Frank	Flo	Filene	Farrah	Foster
Atlantic	Atlantic	Atlantic	Atlantic	Atlantic
Pacific	Pacific	Pacific	Pacific	Pacific
Indian	Indian	Indian	Indian	Indian
Red Sea	Red Sea	Red Sea	Red Sea	Red Sea
Java Sea	Java Sea	Java Sea	Java Sea	Java Sea
Yellow	Yellow	Yellow	Yellow	Yellow
Green	Green	Green	Green	Green
Black	Black	Black	Black	Black
Brown	Brown	Brown	Brown	Brown
Purple	Purple	Purple	Purple	Purple
15 in	15 in	15 in	15 in	15 in
14 in	14 in	14 in	14 in	14 in
13 in	13 in	13 in	13 in	13 in
12 in	12 in	12 in	12 in	12 in
10 in	10 in	10 in	10 in	10 in
10 Years	10 Years	10 Years	10 Years	10 Years
9 Years	9 Years	9 Years	9 Years	9 Years
7 Years	7 Years	7 Years	7 Years	7 Years
5 Years	5 Years	5 Years	5 Years	5 Years
4 Years	4 Years	4 Years	4 Years	4 Years

THE CLUES

1. The 2 frogfish living in the Red Sea and the Java Sea were either black or purple, were the 2 shortest frogfish and were the 2 oldest frogfish.
2. The 2 frogfish living in Atlantic and Indian Oceans were either yellow or green, were the 2 longest frogfish, and were the 2 youngest frogfish.
3. Flo was 2 years older than Frank and Flo was 2 years younger than Farrah.
4. Foster wasn't either black or purple and the yellow frogfish lived in the Indian Ocean but was not the longest frogfish.
5. Frank wasn't green and Farrah wasn't purple.
6. The black frogfish did not live in the Java Sea because the frogfish living in the Java Sea was the shortest frogfish.

THE FACTS

Stingrays are easily identified because of their wide flat bodies equipped with a thin long tail tipped with a poisonous barb. Some rays can grow quite large to over 6 feet in length with a weight of 750 pounds or so but more commonly, they are around 36 inches and less than 50 pounds. When a stingray uses its stinger, the poison barb breaks off but they aren't stinger less for long as the barb soon grows back. The stingray will typically lie on the ocean floor, agitate the sand and hide beneath this covering. The stingray subsists on a diet of snails, clams, oysters, barnacles, shrimp, worms, and small fish. The stingray has two powerful shell-crushing plates in its mouth ideal for such a hard-shelled diet. The chief predator of the stingray is any of several species of shark but stingrays are edible and many humans enjoy eating them as well. Escaping sharks and the frying pan, stingrays can expect to live about 25 years. Sam, Sara, Spike, Sylvia, and Shari were 5 stingrays who were different ages and recently ate a different number of food items. Based on the clues, solve the puzzle.

Sam	Sara	Spike	Sylvia	Shari
20 Years Old	20 Years Old	20 Years Old	20 Years Old	20 Years Old
18 Years Old	18 Years Old	18 Years Old	18 Years Old	18 Years Old
16 Years Old	16 Years Old	16 Years Old	16 Years Old	16 Years Old
15 Years Old	15 Years Old	15 Years Old	15 Years Old	15 Years Old
12 Years Old	12 Years Old	12 Years Old	12 Years Old	12 Years Old
20 Clams	20 Clams	20 Clams	20 Clams	20 Clams
18 Clams	18 Clams	18 Clams	18 Clams	18 Clams
16 Clams	16 Clams	16 Clams	16 Clams	16 Clams
13 Clams	13 Clams	13 Clams	13 Clams	13 Clams
12 Clams	12 Clams	12 Clams	12 Clams	12 Clams
16 Oysters	16 Oysters	16 Oysters	16 Oysters	16 Oysters
13 Oysters	13 Oysters	13 Oysters	13 Oysters	13 Oysters
12 Oysters	12 Oysters	12 Oysters	12 Oysters	12 Oysters
11 Oysters	11 Oysters	11 Oysters	11 Oysters	11 Oysters
10 Oysters	10 Oysters	10 Oysters	10 Oysters	10 Oysters
13 Snails	13 Snails	13 Snails	13 Snails	13 Snails
12 Snails	12 Snails	12 Snails	12 Snails	12 Snails
11 Snails	11 Snails	11 Snails	11 Snails	11 Snails
10 Snails	10 Snails	10 Snails	10 Snails	10 Snails
9 Snails	9 Snails	9 Snails	9 Snails	9 Snails

THE CLUES

1. The 3 oldest stingray clam consumption numbers exactly matched their age numbers while the youngest stingray's age number exactly matched its clam, oyster, and snail numbers.
2. Spike is 2 years younger than Sam but Spike is 3 years older than Sylvia, and Sara wasn't the youngest stingray.
3. Sam ate exactly the same number of oysters and snails but so did both Sara and Sylvia eat the same number of oysters and snails.
4. Sam ate 1 more oyster than Sylvia.

THE FACTS

There are some 95 species of parrotfish found in tropical and subtropical salt water throughout the world. They inhabit coral reefs, rocky reefs, and seagrass beds where they can find their primary food of algae. They get their name from their mouths which are specially adapted for scraping algae off of reefs or rocks and resemble a parrot's beak. Some species of parrotfish can grow quite large but more commonly they are between 12 and 20 inches long. At night, when parrotfish go to sleep, they cover themselves with a mucus sleeping bag they extrude from their mouths. This mucus is believed to hide their scent from predators and keep parasites from infesting them. When parrotfish scrape algae from reefs, they swallow some of the reef which they excrete as sand. Parrotfish have a lifespan of about 7 years in the wild. Petra, Pete, Pilar, Patty, and Paul were 5 parrotfish who lived near different islands, preferred different depths, were different lengths, and were different ages. Based on the clues, solve the puzzle.

Petra	Pete	Pilar	Patty	Paul
Aruba	Aruba	Aruba	Aruba	Aruba
Cuba	Cuba	Cuba	Cuba	Cuba
Puerto Rico	Puerto Rico	Puerto Rico	Puerto Rico	Puerto Rico
Trinidad	Trinidad	Trinidad	Trinidad	Trinidad
Bermuda	Bermuda	Bermuda	Bermuda	Bermuda
20 ft	20 ft	20 ft	20 ft	20 ft
18 ft	18 ft	18 ft	18 ft	18 ft
17 ft	17 ft	17 ft	17 ft	17 ft
16 ft	16 ft	16 ft	16 ft	16 ft
15 ft	15 ft	15 ft	15 ft	15 ft
20 in long	20 in long	20 in long	20 in long	20 in long
18 in long	18 in long	18 in long	18 in long	18 in long
17 in long	17 in long	17 in long	17 in long	17 in long
16 in long	16 in long	16 in long	16 in long	16 in long
15 in long	15 in long	15 in long	15 in long	15 in long
7 Years	7 Years	7 Years	7 Years	7 Years
6 Years	6 Years	6 Years	6 Years	6 Years
5 Years	5 Years	5 Years	5 Years	5 Years
4 Years	4 Years	4 Years	4 Years	4 Years
3 Years	3 Years	3 Years	3 Years	3 Years

THE CLUES

1. The 2 oldest parrotfish were the only fish who had exactly matching favorite depth and length numbers and neither of them lived near Aruba, Puerto Rico, or Trinidad.
2. Petra and Pete did not live near Aruba, Cuba, or Bermuda.
3. Pilar was 1 year older than Patty who was 1 year older than Paul.
4. The parrotfish who enjoyed life at a depth of 20 feet lived near Trinidad and Pete enjoyed life 2 feet deeper than Petra.
5. Pilar didn't live near Cuba, Petra didn't live near Trinidad, and Pilar was 1 inch longer than Patty while Paul was longer than Patty.
6. The youngest parrotfish was the longest. The shortest parrotfish lived at the deepest depth.

Iberian Lynx

THE FACTS

Although closely related to other lynxes found in North America and Asia, the Iberian lynx is considered a separate species. The primary nations on the Iberian Peninsula are Spain and Portugal. The Iberian lynx has the tufted ears, long legs, short tail, and the beard typical of other lynxes around the world. This cat has a head and body length of 33 to 43 inches, a short tail of an additional 4 to 10 inches, and are 24 to 25 inches tall at the shoulder. They weigh between 28 to 59 pounds. Their preferred habitat is shrub land with abundant grass to support its favorite prey of the European rabbit. The lynx is a solitary hunter who will wait patiently for hours until a prey comes near enough for the lynx to pounce. The female lynx has to search out a male if she wishes to breed. Female lynxes will give birth to a litter of 2 to 3 kittens who will stay with her for at least a year. Surviving infanthood and all the other hazards facing the Iberian lynx, it will have a lifespan of about 13 years in the wild. Iris, Irene, Ingo, Ivan, and Ilsa were 5 Iberian lynxes who were different lengths and weights who ate a different number of rabbits in a week and were different ages. Based on the clues, solve the puzzle.

Iris	Irene	Ingo	Ivan	Ilsa
43 in	43 in	43 in	43 in	43 in
42 in	42 in	42 in	42 in	42 in
41 in	41 in	41 in	41 in	41 in
40 in	40 in	40 in	40 in	40 in
39 in	39 in	39 in	39 in	39 in
43 lbs	43 lbs	43 lbs	43 lbs	43 lbs
42 lbs	42 lbs	42 lbs	42 lbs	42 lbs
41 lbs	41 lbs	41 lbs	41 lbs	41 lbs
40 lbs	40 lbs	40 lbs	40 lbs	40 lbs
39 lbs	39 lbs	39 lbs	39 lbs	39 lbs
10 Rabbits	10 Rabbits	10 Rabbits	10 Rabbits	10 Rabbits
9 Rabbits	9 Rabbits	9 Rabbits	9 Rabbits	9 Rabbits
8 Rabbits	8 Rabbits	8 Rabbits	8 Rabbits	8 Rabbits
6 Rabbits	6 Rabbits	6 Rabbits	6 Rabbits	6 Rabbits
4 Rabbits	4 Rabbits	4 Rabbits	4 Rabbits	4 Rabbits
10 Years	10 Years	10 Years	10 Years	10 Years
9 Years	9 Years	9 Years	9 Years	9 Years
8 Years	8 Years	8 Years	8 Years	8 Years
6 Years	6 Years	6 Years	6 Years	6 Years
4 Years	4 Years	4 Years	4 Years	4 Years

THE CLUES

1. By an amazing coincidence, each lynx had matching length and weight numbers and each lynx had matching rabbit consumption and age numbers.
2. Iris was 1 year older than Ingo and Ilsa ate 2 more rabbits than Irene.
3. Ivan was 1 inch longer than Iris and Iris weighed 1 pound more than Ilsa.
4. The heaviest lynx ate 6 rabbits and Irene was older than Ivan.
5. Ingo was 1 inch longer than Ivan.

THE FACTS

The tailless tenrec is also known as the common tenrec but it isn't all that common found only on Madagascar, the Comoros, Mauritius, Reunion, or the Seychelles which are all islands or island chains. The tailless tenrec looks something like a hedgehog, is between 10 to 16 inches long, and weighs between 48 to 96 ounces. The tailless tenrec sleeps in hiding during the day and hunts at night. Its diet consists of all types of Insects, worms, snails, frogs, and mice. If disturbed, this creature will let out a blood-curdling scream, erect its spiny hair, jump back, and try to bite whatever it can. The tenrec is the only known mammal living in a tropical climate with the ability to go into hibernation for up to 9 months a year. Tailless tenrecs have a lifespan of up to 10 years in the wild. Tess, Tina, Tom, Troy, and Tanya were 5 tailless tenrecs who lived on different islands and were different lengths, weights, and ages. Based on the clues, solve the puzzle.

Tess	Tina	Tom	Troy	Tanya
16 ft	16 ft	16 ft	16 ft	16 ft
15 ft	15 ft	15 ft	15 ft	15 ft
14 ft	14 ft	14 ft	14 ft	14 ft
13 ft	13 ft	13 ft	13 ft	13 ft
12 ft	12 ft	12 ft	12 ft	12 ft
3500 lbs	3500 lbs	3500 lbs	3500 lbs	3500 lbs
3400 lbs	3400 lbs	3400 lbs	3400 lbs	3400 lbs
3350 lbs	3350 lbs	3350 lbs	3350 lbs	3350 lbs
3300 lbs	3300 lbs	3300 lbs	3300 lbs	3300 lbs
3250 lbs	3250 lbs	3250 lbs	3250 lbs	3250 lbs
40 Years	40 Years	40 Years	40 Years	40 Years
38 Years	38 Years	38 Years	38 Years	38 Years
36 Years	36 Years	36 Years	36 Years	36 Years
35 Years	35 Years	35 Years	35 Years	35 Years
33 Years	33 Years	33 Years	33 Years	33 Years
Cod	Cod	Cod	Cod	Cod
Halibut	Halibut	Halibut	Halibut	Halibut
Shrimp	Shrimp	Shrimp	Shrimp	Shrimp
Crab	Crab	Crab	Crab	Crab
Squid	Squid	Squid	Squid	Squid

THE CLUES

1. The oldest lived on Madagascar, the heaviest lived on Comoros, the youngest lived on Mauritius, and the 14-inch long tenrec lived on Reunion Island.
2. Tess's length number is exactly twice as large as her age number but the same statement is true for Tina and Tanya.
3. Tina was 1 year older than Tanya and Tanya weighed 4 ounces more than Troy and Tanya wasn't the youngest.
4. Tom was older than Troy, and Tess weighed 4 ounces more than Tom.
5. Troy did not weigh the least and Troy wasn't the shortest tailless tenrec either.
6. Tanya did not live on Comoros.

THE FACTS

The boa constrictor is a large, non-poisonous, heavy-bodied snake native to South and Central America as well as several Caribbean islands. The term "large" is a relative term because while boa constrictors range from 3 to 14 feet and weigh up to 40 pounds or so, it is small compared to the python. Boa constrictors are solitary creatures and hunt, usually by ambush, at night. Their prey includes rats, mice, bats, frogs, rabbits, and bigger prey such as young wild pigs, monkeys, and even the odd ocelot or two. The boa constrictor kills by wrapping its body around its prey so tightly that its victim cannot breathe and dies. The boa then unhinges its jaw and swallows its prey whole. Boa constrictors have a relatively long lifespan of about 30 years. Carl, Connie, Cora, Cathy, and Craig were 5 boa constrictors from different countries who were different lengths, had different favorite foods, and were different ages. Based on the clues, solve the puzzle.

Carl	Connie	Cora	Cathy	Craig
Mexico	Mexico	Mexico	Mexico	Mexico
Panama	Panama	Panama	Panama	Panama
Brazil	Brazil	Brazil	Brazil	Brazil
Bolivia	Bolivia	Bolivia	Bolivia	Bolivia
Venezuela	Venezuela	Venezuela	Venezuela	Venezuela
14 ft	14 ft	14 ft	14 ft	14 ft
13 ft	13 ft	13 ft	13 ft	13 ft
12 ft	12 ft	12 ft	12 ft	12 ft
10 ft	10 ft	10 ft	10 ft	10 ft
9 ft	9 ft	9 ft	9 ft	9 ft
Rat	Rat	Rat	Rat	Rat
Bat	Bat	Bat	Bat	Bat
Monkey	Monkey	Monkey	Monkey	Monkey
Lizard	Lizard	Lizard	Lizard	Lizard
Pig	Pig	Pig	Pig	Pig
28 Years Old	28 Years Old	28 Years Old	28 Years Old	28 Years Old
26 Years Old	26 Years Old	26 Years Old	26 Years Old	26 Years Old
24 Years Old	24 Years Old	24 Years Old	24 Years Old	24 Years Old
20 Years Old	20 Years Old	20 Years Old	20 Years Old	20 Years Old
18 Years Old	18 Years Old	18 Years Old	18 Years Old	18 Years Old

THE CLUES

1. Each snake's feet number is exactly ½ as large as its age number.
2. The two oldest snakes lived in Mexico and Panama and the two youngest snakes lived in Bolivia and Venezuela.
3. The Mexico snake loved to eat rats, the Bolivia snake enjoyed tasty bats, the Panama snake enjoyed a banana flavored monkey best of all, and the Venezuela snake enjoyed the taste of lizard above all.
4. Carl wasn't the longest snake, but he was 1 foot longer than Connie who wasn't the shortest snake, and, of course, Cathy was 1 foot longer than Craig.
5. The youngest snake loved bats, the oldest snake loved rats, and both Connie and Carl did not live in Venezuela.
6. Connie did not live in Panama.

THE FACTS

Weasels are related to ferrets, minks, badgers, otters, and even the fearsome wolverine. The weasel has the distinction of being the smallest mammal carnivore on the planet. Weasels have slender bodies about 6 to 9 inches long. They have 4 short legs tipped with 5 toes all possessing sharp claws. Their body shape enables them to enter burrows and attack burrowing animals. Despite its small size, the weasel is a bold and aggressive hunter able to kill animals more than twice its size. Weasels regularly attack and kill rabbits, shrews, mice, rats, voles, squirrels, chipmunks, frogs, and birds as large as chickens. Weasels do not have the ability to store energy in the form of fat so it must eat frequently. Weasels can run at speeds of about 15 mph and have a normal lifespan of about 30 months. Willy, Wanda, Wayne, Walt, and Wendy were 5 weasels who were different ages and in a recent week escaped from a different predator and ate a different number of rats and mice. Based on the clues, solve the puzzle.

Willy	Wanda	Wayne	Walt	Wendy
30 Months	30 Months	30 Months	30 Months	30 Months
28 Months	28 Months	28 Months	28 Months	28 Months
24 Months	24 Months	24 Months	24 Months	24 Months
20 Months	20 Months	20 Months	20 Months	20 Months
16 Months	16 Months	16 Months	16 Months	16 Months
Hawk	Hawk	Hawk	Hawk	Hawk
Owl	Owl	Owl	Owl	Owl
Fox	Fox	Fox	Fox	Fox
Coyote	Coyote	Coyote	Coyote	Coyote
Snake	Snake	Snake	Snake	Snake
10 Rats	10 Rats	10 Rats	10 Rats	10 Rats
9 Rats	9 Rats	9 Rats	9 Rats	9 Rats
8 Rats	8 Rats	8 Rats	8 Rats	8 Rats
7 Rats	7 Rats	7 Rats	7 Rats	7 Rats
6 Rats	6 Rats	6 Rats	6 Rats	6 Rats
10 Mice	10 Mice	10 Mice	10 Mice	10 Mice
9 Mice	9 Mice	9 Mice	9 Mice	9 Mice
8 Mice	8 Mice	8 Mice	8 Mice	8 Mice
7 Mice	7 Mice	7 Mice	7 Mice	7 Mice
6 Mice	6 Mice	6 Mice	6 Mice	6 Mice

THE CLUES

1. The weasel who ate the most rats ate the fewest mice, the weasel who ate 9 rats ate 7 mice, the weasel who ate 8 rats ate 8 mice, and the weasel who ate 7 rats ate 9 mice.
2. The oldest weasel escaped from a fox, the 28-month old escaped from a hawk, the 24-month old escaped from a snake, and the 20-month old escaped from a coyote.
3. Wendy was 4 months younger than Walt, Walt did not have a narrow escape from a hawk, and Walt was 4 months younger than the weasel who escaped from a snake.
4. Wanda is 4 months older than Wayne and Wendy ate 1 more rat than Walt but Wendy did not eat the most rats.
5. Wayne ate 1 more rat than Wanda but Wayne did not eat the most rats and Wendy ate 1 more mouse than Willy.

Monkfish

THE FACTS

The monkfish is also known as the "frog fish" from its habit of using its pectoral and ventral fins as legs as it crawls around the ocean. The monkfish is composed of a huge head with large jaws filled with inward slanting sharp teeth. Anything entering those jaws can only go down to the monkfish's expandable stomach. The monkfish hides on the ocean floor in sand or seaweed waiting for suitable prey to approach. The monkfish has fringed appendages on its body which have the look of seaweed making the monkfish appear harmless. Monkfish are opportunistic feeders and will dine on anything that will fit in its mouth including sardines, herring, mackerel, snapper, shrimp, crabs, lobsters, and anything else that may come along. Monkfish grow to between 36 to 60 inches and have a normal lifespan of about 15 years. Morrie, Manny, Marie, Mame, and Mona were 5 monkfish who were different ages and lengths and in one week ate a different number of herring and sardines. Based on the clues, solve the puzzle.

Morrie	Manny	Marie	Mame	Mona
15 Years Old	15 Years Old	15 Years Old	15 Years Old	15 Years Old
14 Years Old	14 Years Old	14 Years Old	14 Years Old	14 Years Old
12 Years Old	12 Years Old	12 Years Old	12 Years Old	12 Years Old
11 Years Old	11 Years Old	11 Years Old	11 Years Old	11 Years Old
10 Years Old	10 Years Old	10 Years Old	10 Years Old	10 Years Old
60 in	60 in	60 in	60 in	60 in
58 in	58 in	58 in	58 in	58 in
55 in	55 in	55 in	55 in	55 in
53 in	53 in	53 in	53 in	53 in
50 in	50 in	50 in	50 in	50 in
30 Herring	30 Herring	30 Herring	30 Herring	30 Herring
29 Herring	29 Herring	29 Herring	29 Herring	29 Herring
28 Herring	28 Herring	28 Herring	28 Herring	28 Herring
25 Herring	25 Herring	25 Herring	25 Herring	25 Herring
20 Herring	20 Herring	20 Herring	20 Herring	20 Herring
25 Sardines	25 Sardines	25 Sardines	25 Sardines	25 Sardines
20 Sardines	20 Sardines	20 Sardines	20 Sardines	20 Sardines
18 Sardines	18 Sardines	18 Sardines	18 Sardines	18 Sardines
15 Sardines	15 Sardines	15 Sardines	15 Sardines	15 Sardines
10 Sardines	10 Sardines	10 Sardines	10 Sardines	10 Sardines

THE CLUES

1. Morrie and Mame were not the oldest or the longest monkfish and Morrie ate the same number of herring and sardines and Mame also ate the same number of herring and sardines.
2. Manny's inches number is twice as large as his herring number but Mona's inches number is twice as large as her herring number and Mame's inches number is twice as large as her herring number.
3. The oldest monkfish ate the most herring, the youngest monkfish ate the fewest herring, and Mame was 1 year older than Mona.
4. Morrie is shorter than Marie.
5. Manny ate 5 more sardines than Mona.

THE FACTS

The climbing perch is a member of the "labyrinth" fish native to Southeast Asia. Labyrinth fishes all have a chamber over their gills that enables them to absorb and retain atmospheric oxygen. When walking, this fish walks with a jerky movement as it propels itself along with its fins and tail. The usual reason for this fish to take a stroll is to find a new pond if the old pond dries up. The walking fish can live for several days without water and can also dig into the mud of dried up stream beds and survive for up to 6 months. This fish is brown and up to 25 centimeters in length. Despite its small size, the climbing perch is deadly to any fish, bird, or animal who swallows it whole as it has a trick of swelling itself up and blocking the throat of its predator. Unable to eat or breathe, the predator soon dies of what turned out to be a bad seafood dinner. Cecil, Carl, Chandra, Cindy, and Cassie were 5 climbing perch who lived in different bodies of water, were different, lengths, walked different distances, and were out of water for a different number of days. Based on the clues, solve the puzzle.

Cecil	Carl	Chandra	Cindy	Cassie
Puddle	Puddle	Puddle	Puddle	Puddle
Pond	Pond	Pond	Pond	Pond
Stream	Stream	Stream	Stream	Stream
River	River	River	River	River
Lake	Lake	Lake	Lake	Lake
25 cm	25 cm	25 cm	25 cm	25 cm
24 cm	24 cm	24 cm	24 cm	24 cm
23 cm	23 cm	23 cm	23 cm	23 cm
22 cm	22 cm	22 cm	22 cm	22 cm
21 cm	21 cm	21 cm	21 cm	21 cm
10,000 ft	10,000 ft	10,000 ft	10,000 ft	10,000 ft
9,500 ft	9,500 ft	9,500 ft	9,500 ft	9,500 ft
9,300 ft	9,300 ft	9,300 ft	9,300 ft	9,300 ft
9,100 ft	9,100 ft	9,100 ft	9,100 ft	9,100 ft
8,900 ft	8,900 ft	8,900 ft	8,900 ft	8,900 ft
8 Days	8 Days	8 Days	8 Days	8 Days
7 Days	7 Days	7 Days	7 Days	7 Days
6 Days	6 Days	6 Days	6 Days	6 Days
5 Days	5 Days	5 Days	5 Days	5 Days
4 Days	4 Days	4 Days	4 Days	4 Days

THE CLUES

1. The longest fish lived in a river, the 2nd longest fish lived in a stream, the 3rd longest fish lived in a lake, and the shortest fish lived in a puddle.
2. Chandra walked 200 feet less than Carl, Chandra also walked 200 feet farther than Cindy.
3. Cassie did not live in a stream, river or lake and Cassie was longer than Carl and Cassie did not walk as far as Cindy.
4. The puddle-living fish was out of water the most days and the longest fish was only out of the water 4 days.
5. Cindy did not live in a river and Cecil was 1 centimeter shorter than the stream living fish.
6. Cassie was out of water 1 day less than Carl, but Cassie was out of water 1 day more than Cecil.

THE FACTS

Swans are the largest members of the waterfowl family and are among the largest flying birds found anywhere. The 3 larger species of swans are the mute, trumpeter, and whooper. All three species can reach 60 inches in length and weigh as much as 33 pounds. Swans prefer a temperate climate and will migrate as the seasons change to maintain a temperate climate year-round. No birds, including swans, have teeth but swans do have serrated beaks which function much like teeth as they feed on both land and water. Swans have long been celebrated as symbols of love and fidelity because they mate for life and both males and females participate in building a nest, incubating the 3 to 8 eggs the female lays, and protecting and raising their young. Swans can have a lifespan of 20 years or so. Sally, Sarah, Sheena, Sophie, and Sybil were 5 female swans who were different lengths, weights, and ages and laid a different number of eggs. Based on the clues, solve the puzzle.

Sally	Sarah	Sheena	Sophie	Sybil
60 in	60 in	60 in	60 in	60 in
58 in	58 in	58 in	58 in	58 in
57 in	57 in	57 in	57 in	57 in
56 in	56 in	56 in	56 in	56 in
54 in	54 in	54 in	54 in	54 in
33 lbs	33 lbs	33 lbs	33 lbs	33 lbs
32 lbs	32 lbs	32 lbs	32 lbs	32 lbs
31 lbs	31 lbs	31 lbs	31 lbs	31 lbs
30 lbs	30 lbs	30 lbs	30 lbs	30 lbs
29 lbs	29 lbs	29 lbs	29 lbs	29 lbs
15 Years Old	15 Years Old	15 Years Old	15 Years Old	15 Years Old
13 Years Old	13 Years Old	13 Years Old	13 Years Old	13 Years Old
12 Years Old	12 Years Old	12 Years Old	12 Years Old	12 Years Old
10 Years Old	10 Years Old	10 Years Old	10 Years Old	10 Years Old
9 Years Old	9 Years Old	9 Years Old	9 Years Old	9 Years Old
8 Eggs	8 Eggs	8 Eggs	8 Eggs	8 Eggs
7 Eggs	7 Eggs	7 Eggs	7 Eggs	7 Eggs
6 Eggs	6 Eggs	6 Eggs	6 Eggs	6 Eggs
5 Eggs	5 Eggs	5 Eggs	5 Eggs	5 Eggs
4 Eggs	4 Eggs	4 Eggs	4 Eggs	4 Eggs

THE CLUES

1. Sheena's inches number is exactly twice as large as her pounds number but the same statement is true for Sophie as well.
2. Sarah's age number is exactly twice as large as her egg number but the same statement is true for Sally as well.
3. The oldest swan weighed the least and the youngest swan weighed 31 pounds.
4. The shortest swan weighed the most and laid 5 eggs.
5. Sophie laid 1 more egg than Sarah, Sophie laid more eggs than Sheena, and Sheena weighed more than Sophie.
6. Sheena was older than Sarah, Sarah was longer than Sally but shorter than Sybil, and Sarah weighed 1 pound more than Sybil.

THE FACTS

The anaconda is a large non-poisonous snake native to tropical areas of South America. Anaconda's can reach lengths of 30 feet or so and can weigh upwards of 500 pounds. Anacondas prefer to spend most of their time submerged in water with only their eyes and nostrils sticking out. They are lying in wait for suitable prey to happen along. Such prey may include rodents, fish, birds, caimans, capybaras, tapirs, and deer. Anacondas kill their prey by squeezing it until it can no longer sense a heartbeat. Female anacondas give birth to live offspring in litters of 20 to 40 young who are all about 2 feet long and able to swim and hunt immediately. Arnie, Alex, April, Annie, and Art were 5 anacondas from 5 different countries who were different lengths and weights and had a different favorite meal. Based on the clues, solve the puzzle.

Arnie	Alex	April	Annie	Art
Columbia	Columbia	Columbia	Columbia	Columbia
Ecuador	Ecuador	Ecuador	Ecuador	Ecuador
Peru	Peru	Peru	Peru	Peru
Bolivia	Bolivia	Bolivia	Bolivia	Bolivia
Brazil	Brazil	Brazil	Brazil	Brazil
32 ft	32 ft	32 ft	32 ft	32 ft
31 ft	31 ft	31 ft	31 ft	31 ft
29 ft	29 ft	29 ft	29 ft	29 ft
27 ft	27 ft	27 ft	27 ft	27 ft
25 ft	25 ft	25 ft	25 ft	25 ft
500 lbs	500 lbs	500 lbs	500 lbs	500 lbs
490 lbs	490 lbs	490 lbs	490 lbs	490 lbs
460 lbs	460 lbs	460 lbs	460 lbs	460 lbs
450 lbs	450 lbs	450 lbs	450 lbs	450 lbs
400 lbs	400 lbs	400 lbs	400 lbs	400 lbs
Deer	Deer	Deer	Deer	Deer
Tapir	Tapir	Tapir	Tapir	Tapir
Monkey	Monkey	Monkey	Monkey	Monkey
Capybara	Capybara	Capybara	Capybara	Capybara
Caiman	Caiman	Caiman	Caiman	Caiman

THE CLUES

1. The longest and the shortest anacondas were from either Peru or Bolivia, had favorite foods of either deer or tapir, and one was the heaviest and the other was the lightest.
2. The 2nd longest anaconda lived in Brazil, was the 2nd heaviest anaconda, and loved to eat fat monkeys.
3. The 3rd longest anaconda lived in Ecuador, was the 3rd heaviest snake at 460 pounds, and loved to eat caimans best of all.
4. Art was 2 feet longer than Alex, Annie was 2 feet longer than Art, and Annie didn't like to eat either tapir or deer.
5. Annie and April did not live in Brazil, Art was longer than the heaviest snake from Bolivia.
6. The longest anaconda's favorite food was not deer.

Dall Sheep

THE FACTS

Dall sheep are found only in the dry mountainous regions of Alaska, the Yukon, the Northwest Territories, and British Columbia. Dall sheep are pure white, weigh between 100 to 240 pounds, and rarely exceed 5 feet or so in length. Dall sheep predators include wolves, coyotes, lynx, grizzlies, black bears, wolverines, and eagles will take very young Dall sheep. During the summer, male Dall sheep, known as rams, take the time to establish dominance to determine who will be allowed to breed. Usually the ram with the bigger horns will be the automatic winner. Dall sheep have a lifespan of about 12 years. Dave, Deedee, Dian, Dylan, and Danny were 5 Dall sheep who preferred to live at different heights, had a close call with a different predator, and were different weights and ages. Based on the clues, solve the puzzle.

Dave	Deedee	Dian	Dylan	Danny
10,000 ft	10,000 ft	10,000 ft	10,000 ft	10,000 ft
9,500 ft	9,500 ft	9,500 ft	9,500 ft	9,500 ft
9,000 ft	9,000 ft	9,000 ft	9,000 ft	9,000 ft
8,500 ft	8,500 ft	8,500 ft	8,500 ft	8,500 ft
8,000 ft	8,000 ft	8,000 ft	8,000 ft	8,000 ft
Wolf	Wolf	Wolf	Wolf	Wolf
Coyote	Coyote	Coyote	Coyote	Coyote
Lynx	Lynx	Lynx	Lynx	Lynx
Grizzly	Grizzly	Grizzly	Grizzly	Grizzly
Eagle	Eagle	Eagle	Eagle	Eagle
250 lbs	250 lbs	250 lbs	250 lbs	250 lbs
230 lbs	230 lbs	230 lbs	230 lbs	230 lbs
210 lbs	210 lbs	210 lbs	210 lbs	210 lbs
200 lbs	200 lbs	200 lbs	200 lbs	200 lbs
180 lbs	180 lbs	180 lbs	180 lbs	180 lbs
12 Years Old	12 Years Old	12 Years Old	12 Years Old	12 Years Old
11 Years Old	11 Years Old	11 Years Old	11 Years Old	11 Years Old
9 Years Old	9 Years Old	9 Years Old	9 Years Old	9 Years Old
7 Years Old	7 Years Old	7 Years Old	7 Years Old	7 Years Old
5 Years Old	5 Years Old	5 Years Old	5 Years Old	5 Years Old

THE CLUES

1. The youngest weighed the least, was chased by a wolf, and lived at the highest elevation.
2. The oldest weighed 200 pounds, was chased by a coyote, and lived at 9,500 feet.
3. Dave, who wasn't chased by either a wolf or a coyote, lived 500 feet higher than Dylan who wasn't chased by a lynx or an eagle.
4. The 9 year old sheep lived at the lowest elevation, weighed the most, and was chased by a grizzly.
5. Danny wasn't chased by an eagle, and Danny was 2 years older than Deedee, and Dave weighed more than Danny.

THE FACTS

Flamingos are pink wading birds with long thin legs who can be anywhere between 3 to 5 feet tall and weigh between 2 ½ to 8 pounds. Flamingos are famous for always standing on one leg and it was thought they did this to conserve body heat while feeding in cold water. This was common wisdom until some smarty-pants pointed out that they stand on one leg in warm water too. Flamingos feed themselves with a process called "filter-feeding" using specially adapted beaks which can separate mud and silt from the plant and animal plankton they feed on. Flamingos are excellent fliers and can fly at speeds up to 35 mph for hundreds of miles in one day. Flamingos are very social animals and live in colonies of thousands. At breeding time, paired couples will build a nest together and take turns incubating their eggs. Both parents feed their young "crop milk" until their young leave their tender loving care after only 2 weeks. The parent flamingos have no further role in raising their young. Flamingos have a long lifespan of 25 to 30 years in the wild. Fanny, Frank, Flo, Ferris, and Finley were 5 flamingos who were different heights and weights, who had different top speeds, and were different ages. Based on the clues, solve the puzzle.

Fanny	Frank	Flo	Ferris	Finley
45 in	45 in	45 in	45 in	45 in
43 in	43 in	43 in	43 in	43 in
40 in	40 in	40 in	40 in	40 in
38 in	38 in	38 in	38 in	38 in
35 in	35 in	35 in	35 in	35 in
90 oz	90 oz	90 oz	90 oz	90 oz
86 oz	86 oz	86 oz	86 oz	86 oz
80 oz	80 oz	80 oz	80 oz	80 oz
75 oz	75 oz	75 oz	75 oz	75 oz
70 oz	70 oz	70 oz	70 oz	70 oz
35 mph	35 mph	35 mph	35 mph	35 mph
34 mph	34 mph	34 mph	34 mph	34 mph
33 mph	33 mph	33 mph	33 mph	33 mph
32 mph	32 mph	32 mph	32 mph	32 mph
31 mph	31 mph	31 mph	31 mph	31 mph
20 Years	20 Years	20 Years	20 Years	20 Years
18 Years	18 Years	18 Years	18 Years	18 Years
17 Years	17 Years	17 Years	17 Years	17 Years
16 Years	16 Years	16 Years	16 Years	16 Years
15 Years	15 Years	15 Years	15 Years	15 Years

THE CLUES

1. The tallest flamingo weighed the most but was the slowest flyer and the youngest flamingo.
2. The shortest flamingo weighed the least but was the fastest flyer and the oldest flamingo.
3. The 40 inch tall flamingo had the middle number all the way down and weighed 80 ounces, flew 33 mph, and was 17 years old.
4. Fanny weighed 5 ounces more than Ferris, Frank was 1 year older than Fanny and neither Ferris or Finley were less than 18 years old.
5. Frank was shorter than Fanny but Frank flew faster than Fanny.

THE FACTS

The skipjack is a medium-sized bony fish in the tuna family. It is also known as the aku, bonita, striped tuna, and the victor fish. The skipjack prefers warm-temperate waters where it is able to spawn all year long. Skipjack prefer to travel in huge schools of as many as 50,000 fish and during the day they descend to 850 feet or so but at night they swim close to the surface and this is when commercial fishermen using purse nets are able to capture them. Skipjacks have a normal lifespan of up to 12 years or so. In addition to commercial fishermen, the skipjack is a popular gamefish sought by ordinary sports fishing persons. Skippy, Shari, Sheila, Sonny, and Sam were 5 skipjack who were different lengths and weights. They were caught by 5 fisherpersons using 5 different fish as bait. Based on the clues, solve the puzzle.

Skippy	Shari	Sheila	Sonny	Sam
38 in	38 in	38 in	38 in	38 in
37 in	37 in	37 in	37 in	37 in
35 in	35 in	35 in	35 in	35 in
34 in	34 in	34 in	34 in	34 in
32 in	32 in	32 in	32 in	32 in
28 lbs	28 lbs	28 lbs	28 lbs	28 lbs
27 lbs	27 lbs	27 lbs	27 lbs	27 lbs
26 lbs	26 lbs	26 lbs	26 lbs	26 lbs
24 lbs	24 lbs	24 lbs	24 lbs	24 lbs
22 lbs	22 lbs	22 lbs	22 lbs	22 lbs
Tom	Tom	Tom	Tom	Tom
Beth	Beth	Beth	Beth	Beth
Randy	Randy	Randy	Randy	Randy
Ryan	Ryan	Ryan	Ryan	Ryan
Rosie	Rosie	Rosie	Rosie	Rosie
Anchovy	Anchovy	Anchovy	Anchovy	Anchovy
Sardine	Sardine	Sardine	Sardine	Sardine
Herring	Herring	Herring	Herring	Herring
Perch	Perch	Perch	Perch	Perch
Squid	Squid	Squid	Squid	Squid

THE CLUES

1. Oddly, the longest skipjack weighed the least, the 2nd longest weighed 24 pounds, the 3rd longest weighed 26 pounds, and the 34 inch skipjack weighed 27 pounds.

2. Tom caught the longest skipjack using an anchovy as bait, Beth caught the 24 pound skipjack using a squid as bait, and Randy caught the 35 inch skipjack using a herring as bait.

3. Skippy was 2 inches shorter than Sam but Sam weighed 1 pound less than Skippy.

4. Sheila did not get fooled by either the anchovy or herring baits and Sam wasn't caught by Rosie and her sardine bait.

5. Sheila weighed 2 pounds less than Sonny.

THE FACTS

The aardwolf looks remarkably like a down-sized hyena as it should being a close relative of the hyena. Somewhere in the far distant past, the aardwolf branch of the hyena family, decided it didn't much like hunting and eating animals for their meat. instead, the aardwolf family decided eating insects was the best way to survive. The aardwolf specializes in eating termites it catches with a long sticky tongue. Aardwolves can eat as much as 250 thousand termites in one night. Aardwolves range in length from 22 to 31 inches with a bushy tail adding another foot or so. Aardwolves weigh only between 15 to 30 pounds. Aardwolves mate for life and both mates work together to defend their territory. Aardwolves aren't fast runners and when faced with a dangerous predator the aardwolf will raise its mane to appear larger and emit a foul-smelling secretion from its anal glands to smell unappetizing. Aardwolves have a lifespan of 18 years in captivity but less in the wild. Ava, Amy, Arthur, Albert, and Alice ate different totals for termites one recent night and they were different lengths, weights, and ages. Based on the clues, solve the puzzle.

Ava	Amy	Arthur	Albert	Alice
250,000	250,000	250,000	250,000	250,000
245,000	245,000	245,000	245,000	245,000
240,000	240,000	240,000	240,000	240,000
230,000	230,000	230,000	230,000	230,000
225,000	225,000	225,000	225,000	225,000
31 in long	31 in long	31 in long	31 in long	31 in long
30 in long	30 in long	30 in long	30 in long	30 in long
28 in long	28 in long	28 in long	28 in long	28 in long
27 in long	27 in long	27 in long	27 in long	27 in long
25 in long	25 in long	25 in long	25 in long	25 in long
30 lbs	30 lbs	30 lbs	30 lbs	30 lbs
29 lbs	29 lbs	29 lbs	29 lbs	29 lbs
28 lbs	28 lbs	28 lbs	28 lbs	28 lbs
26 lbs	26 lbs	26 lbs	26 lbs	26 lbs
25 lbs	25 lbs	25 lbs	25 lbs	25 lbs
14 Years	14 Years	14 Years	14 Years	14 Years
13 Years	13 Years	13 Years	13 Years	13 Years
12 Years	12 Years	12 Years	12 Years	12 Years
10 Years	10 Years	10 Years	10 Years	10 Years
8 Years	8 Years	8 Years	8 Years	8 Years

THE CLUES

1. The oldest aardwolf ate the most termites, the 2nd oldest ate the 2nd most termites, and the same pattern is true for the 3rd, 4th, and 5th oldest who ate the 3rd, 4th, and 5th most termites.
2. Oddly, 3 aardwolves had exactly matching length and weight numbers and these matching numbers belonged to the 3 youngest aardwolves.
3. Amy is not the oldest aardwolf but it is 1 year older than Arthur but Amy is younger than Ava.
4. Albert ate more termites than Alice and Alice weighed 1 pound more than Ava.
5. Ava wasn't the longest aardwolf but Ava was longer than Albert.

THE FACTS

The avocet is a large wading bird with long thin legs, webbed feet, and has black and white plumage. It can only survive in temperate climates and depending on the season the American avocet will be found in Southern Canada, Alberta, Saskatchewan, Manitoba, or in the U.S. along the Pacific coasts of Washington, Oregon, and California. When it gets cold, the avocet will migrate south. The avocet is about 15 to 20 inches long, 25 to 30 inches tall, and weighs between 9 to 15 ounces. During breeding season, males splash water on themselves to attract females. Once a female has chosen a splashy mate, the pair will settle down with large flocks of other avocets to incubate and hatch the four eggs the female lays. As soon as the eggs hatch, the newborn chicks are entirely on their own and are expected to leave the nest within 24 hours. Despite such a challenging childhood, avocets have a reasonable lifespan of 10 to 15 years. Andy, Avis, Astrid, Armin, and Astor were 5 avocets native to 5 locations who were different ages, heights, and weights. Based on the clues, solve the puzzle.

Andy	Avis	Astrid	Armin	Astor
Alberta	Alberta	Alberta	Alberta	Alberta
Manitoba	Manitoba	Manitoba	Manitoba	Manitoba
Texas	Texas	Texas	Texas	Texas
Florida	Florida	Florida	Florida	Florida
Mexico	Mexico	Mexico	Mexico	Mexico
15 Years	15 Years	15 Years	15 Years	15 Years
14 Years	14 Years	14 Years	14 Years	14 Years
13 Years	13 Years	13 Years	13 Years	13 Years
12 Years	12 Years	12 Years	12 Years	12 Years
10 Years	10 Years	10 Years	10 Years	10 Years
30 in	30 in	30 in	30 in	30 in
28 in	28 in	28 in	28 in	28 in
27 in	27 in	27 in	27 in	27 in
26 in	26 in	26 in	26 in	26 in
25 in	25 in	25 in	25 in	25 in
15 oz	15 oz	15 oz	15 oz	15 oz
14 oz	14 oz	14 oz	14 oz	14 oz
13 oz	13 oz	13 oz	13 oz	13 oz
12 oz	12 oz	12 oz	12 oz	12 oz
10 oz	10 oz	10 oz	10 oz	10 oz

THE CLUES

1. The tallest avocet was native to Alberta and the shortest avocet was native to Mexico.
2. The 15 year old was 15 ounces, the 13 year old was 13 ounces, and the 10 year old was 10 ounces but the other 2 avocets did not have matching age and weight numbers.
3. The 3 youngest avocets were native to Texas, Florida, and Mexico.
4. Astrid was 1 year older than Armin, Armin is 1 year older than Andy, and Andy is 1 year older than Astor.
5. Astor was not from Mexico, Andy wasn't from Texas, and Andy was 1 inch taller than Avis.
6. Astor was 1 inch taller than Armin.

THE FACTS

The arrow worm is a tiny predatory marine organism shaped like a torpedo. Ranging in size from an almost microscopic 2 millimeters to 120 millimeters, the arrow worm is a nightmarish predator. It has 4 to 14 hooked spines on either side of its head which are used to drag helpless prey towards its mouth filled with rows of tiny teeth which, to make matters worse, inject a poison called a "tetrode toxin" into the poor victim. If one was to design an eating machine it would probably look like an arrow worm. Arrow worms are hermaphrodites meaning they carry both eggs and sperm in their bodies. When mating, both arrow worms deposit sperm on each other's necks which swim down to the tails where the eggs are located. Arrow worms eat fish larvae, krill, and animal plankton such as copepods, pteropods, and chordates as well as other arrow worms. Wendy, Wilma, Westy, Willy, and Wayne were 5 arrow worms who were different lengths, ate a different number of tiny marine organisms, were different ages, and had a different favorite marine organism to eat. Based on the clues, solve the puzzle.

Wendy	Wilma	Westy	Willy	Wayne
10 Larvae	10 Larvae	10 Larvae	10 Larvae	10 Larvae
9 Larvae	9 Larvae	9 Larvae	9 Larvae	9 Larvae
7 Larvae	7 Larvae	7 Larvae	7 Larvae	7 Larvae
6 Larvae	6 Larvae	6 Larvae	6 Larvae	6 Larvae
5 Larvae	5 Larvae	5 Larvae	5 Larvae	5 Larvae
10 Krill	10 Krill	10 Krill	10 Krill	10 Krill
9 Krill	9 Krill	9 Krill	9 Krill	9 Krill
7 Krill	7 Krill	7 Krill	7 Krill	7 Krill
6 Krill	6 Krill	6 Krill	6 Krill	6 Krill
5 Krill	5 Krill	5 Krill	5 Krill	5 Krill
10 Copepods	10 Copepods	10 Copepods	10 Copepods	10 Copepods
9 Copepods	9 Copepods	9 Copepods	9 Copepods	9 Copepods
7 Copepods	7 Copepods	7 Copepods	7 Copepods	7 Copepods
6 Copepods	6 Copepods	6 Copepods	6 Copepods	6 Copepods
5 Copepods	5 Copepods	5 Copepods	5 Copepods	5 Copepods
10 Pteropods	10 Pteropods	10 Pteropods	10 Pteropods	10 Pteropods
9 Pteropods	9 Pteropods	9 Pteropods	9 Pteropods	9 Pteropods
7 Pteropods	7 Pteropods	7 Pteropods	7 Pteropods	7 Pteropods
6 Pteropods	6 Pteropods	6 Pteropods	6 Pteropods	6 Pteropods
5 Pteropods	5 Pteropods	5 Pteropods	5 Pteropods	5 Pteropods
10 Worms	10 Worms	10 Worms	10 Worms	10 Worms
9 Worms	9 Worms	9 Worms	9 Worms	9 Worms
7 Worms	7 Worms	7 Worms	7 Worms	7 Worms
6 Worms	6 Worms	6 Worms	6 Worms	6 Worms
5 Worms	5 Worms	5 Worms	5 Worms	5 Worms

THE CLUES

1. Wendy and Wilma together ate 15 larvae but Westy and Willy also ate a combined total of 15 larvae.
2. Wendy and Wilma together ate 15 krill and Westy and Wayne together also ate 15 krill.
3. Willy ate 1 more krill than Wilma and 1 more copepod than Wilma as well but Wilma did not eat the fewest copepods.
4. Willy ate 1 more larvae than Wilma and Wayne ate more krill than Wendy. Wilma ate 1 more worm than Willy.
5. Wilma and Westy together ate 15 copepods and together Willy and Wayne ate 15 worms.

Australian Brush Turkey

THE FACTS

The brush turkey is fairly widespread in Australia and will inhabit areas of rainforest but easily tolerates life in drier areas and lately has become satisfied with life in cities. The brush turkey is a fairly large bird with black feathers and a red head. Adult birds achieve lengths of between 23 to 33 inches and weighs up to 5 pounds or so. The brush turkey has a moderate wingspan of only 28 to 33 inches which makes for clumsy flights but useful to escape predators and reach a roost in a tree. Brush turkeys live in communal groups led by a dominant male, one or two younger males, and several females. The male is expected to guard the nest from animals who enjoy eating brush turkey eggs. When the eggs hatch deep inside the mound, the newborn chicks are expected to dig themselves out and begin life without parental support. The brush turkey has a lifespan of up to 25 years in the wild. Beth, Beryl, Birdie, Brin, and Bonnie were 5 female brush turkeys of different ages who laid a different number of eggs and who hatched a different number of male and female chicks. Based on the clues, solve the puzzle.

Beth	Beryl	Birdie	Brin	Bonnie
20 Years Old	20 Years Old	20 Years Old	20 Years Old	20 Years Old
18 Years Old	18 Years Old	18 Years Old	18 Years Old	18 Years Old
17 Years Old	17 Years Old	17 Years Old	17 Years Old	17 Years Old
16 Years Old	16 Years Old	16 Years Old	16 Years Old	16 Years Old
15 Years Old	15 Years Old	15 Years Old	15 Years Old	15 Years Old
20 Eggs	20 Eggs	20 Eggs	20 Eggs	20 Eggs
18 Eggs	18 Eggs	18 Eggs	18 Eggs	18 Eggs
17 Eggs	17 Eggs	17 Eggs	17 Eggs	17 Eggs
16 Eggs	16 Eggs	16 Eggs	16 Eggs	16 Eggs
15 Eggs	15 Eggs	15 Eggs	15 Eggs	15 Eggs
13 Males	13 Males	13 Males	13 Males	13 Males
12 Males	12 Males	12 Males	12 Males	12 Males
11 Males	11 Males	11 Males	11 Males	11 Males
10 Males	10 Males	10 Males	10 Males	10 Males
9 Males	9 Males	9 Males	9 Males	9 Males
9 Females	9 Females	9 Females	9 Females	9 Females
8 Females	8 Females	8 Females	8 Females	8 Females
7 Females	7 Females	7 Females	7 Females	7 Females
5 Females	5 Females	5 Females	5 Females	5 Females
2 Females	2 Females	2 Females	2 Females	2 Females

THE CLUES

1. Oddly, the age numbers and the eggs numbers exactly matched for all five brush turkeys.
2. Brin had 3 more female chicks than Beth but Brin only had 1 more female chick than Bonnie while Birdie had 1 more female chick than Brin.
3. Birdie, Brin, and Bonnie each had exactly 2 more male chicks than female chicks.
4. Beryl was younger than Beth.

Pampas Fox

THE FACTS

The pampas fox is not a true fox and is more closely related to wolves, dogs, jackals, and coyotes than anything in the fox family. The pampas fox is a medium sized animal that has a bushy tail and resembles a coyote more than anything else. Not counting the tail, the pampas fox is usually between 20 to 31 inches long and weighs between 5 and 17 pounds. Native to the vast expanse of grassland called the pampas. The pampas fox can be found in Argentina, Uruguay, Paraguay, Bolivia, and Brazil. The pampas fox lives a nocturnal, solitary life for the most part but during breeding season the foxes form a monogamous bond. The female gives birth to up to 8 kits. The mother and kits stay together in the burrow while the male is kept busy bringing them food. One of the secrets of the pampas foxes' survival is their willingness to eat just about anything including birds, rodents, hares, frogs, fruit, carrion, Insects, lizards, armadillos, snails, eggs, and just about anything else considered remotely edible. The pampas fox has a lifespan of about 14 years. Paul, Pete, Peri, Pela, and Penn were 5 pampas foxes who in one recent night went out and caught and ate a different number of Insects, mice, frogs, and snails. Based on the clues, solve the puzzle.

Paul	Pete	Peri	Pela	Penn
100 Insects	100 Insects	100 Insects	100 Insects	100 Insects
90 Insects	90 Insects	90 Insects	90 Insects	90 Insects
85 Insects	85 Insects	85 Insects	85 Insects	85 Insects
80 Insects	80 Insects	80 Insects	80 Insects	80 Insects
75 Insects	75 Insects	75 Insects	75 Insects	75 Insects
10 Mice	10 Mice	10 Mice	10 Mice	10 Mice
9 Mice	9 Mice	9 Mice	9 Mice	9 Mice
7 Mice	7 Mice	7 Mice	7 Mice	7 Mice
5 Mice	5 Mice	5 Mice	5 Mice	5 Mice
4 Mice	4 Mice	4 Mice	4 Mice	4 Mice
7 Frogs	7 Frogs	7 Frogs	7 Frogs	7 Frogs
6 Frogs	6 Frogs	6 Frogs	6 Frogs	6 Frogs
4 Frogs	4 Frogs	4 Frogs	4 Frogs	4 Frogs
3 Frogs	3 Frogs	3 Frogs	3 Frogs	3 Frogs
2 Frogs	2 Frogs	2 Frogs	2 Frogs	2 Frogs
15 Snails	15 Snails	15 Snails	15 Snails	15 Snails
13 Snails	13 Snails	13 Snails	13 Snails	13 Snails
12 Snails	12 Snails	12 Snails	12 Snails	12 Snails
11 Snails	11 Snails	11 Snails	11 Snails	11 Snails
9 Snails	9 Snails	9 Snails	9 Snails	9 Snails

THE CLUES

1. One pampas fox ate the 2nd largest number of all four food items and each of the others all ate the most of 1 food item and the fewest of another food item.
2. Paul ate 1 more mouse than Peri, Penn ate 2 more mice than Pela, and Pela ate 1 more mouse than Pete.
3. Pela ate 5 more Insects than Paul but Penn ate 5 more Insects than Pela.
4. Pela ate more frogs than Peri, Pete ate 1 more frog than Paul.
5. Pete ate more snails than Paul.

Desert Tortoise

THE FACTS

Native to the Mojave and Sonoran Deserts of Mexico and the states of Arizona, California, Nevada, and Utah, the desert tortoise is also the state reptile of both California and Nevada. Desert tortoises grow very slowly but eventually can obtain a length of 10 to 15 inches and a weight between 24 to 51 pounds. Because of the harsh climate of its habitat, the tortoise spends up to 95% of its time living in burrows either to escape very high or very low temperatures. Finding water, the tortoise will drink enormous quantities of water that it stores in its over-sized bladder. Given the right soil, desert tortoises have the ability to dig their own burrows but seem to prefer using burrows dug by other animals. Often other tortoises will have the same idea and as many as 23 desert tortoises may be found in the same burrow all peacefully hibernating the time away until it rains again. Infant tortoises are a favorite food item of ravens, Gila monsters, foxes, badgers, road runners, coyotes, and even the dreaded fire ants. Surviving all that, desert tortoises have a lifespan of up to 50 years or so. Del, Dolly, Denise, Donald, and Dalia were 5 desert tortoises from different locations who as infants escaped from a different predator and as adults are different weights and ages. Based on the clues, solve the puzzle.

Del	Dolly	Denise	Donald	Dalia
Mexico	Mexico	Mexico	Mexico	Mexico
Arizona	Arizona	Arizona	Arizona	Arizona
California	California	California	California	California
Nevada	Nevada	Nevada	Nevada	Nevada
Utah	Utah	Utah	Utah	Utah
Raven	Raven	Raven	Raven	Raven
Fox	Fox	Fox	Fox	Fox
Badger	Badger	Badger	Badger	Badger
Coyote	Coyote	Coyote	Coyote	Coyote
Gila Monster	Gila Monster	Gila Monster	Gila Monster	Gila Monster
50 lbs	50 lbs	50 lbs	50 lbs	50 lbs
45 lbs	45 lbs	45 lbs	45 lbs	45 lbs
40 lbs	40 lbs	40 lbs	40 lbs	40 lbs
35 lbs	35 lbs	35 lbs	35 lbs	35 lbs
30 lbs	30 lbs	30 lbs	30 lbs	30 lbs
50 Years Old	50 Years Old	50 Years Old	50 Years Old	50 Years Old
45 Years Old	45 Years Old	45 Years Old	45 Years Old	45 Years Old
40 Years Old	40 Years Old	40 Years Old	40 Years Old	40 Years Old
35 Years Old	35 Years Old	35 Years Old	35 Years Old	35 Years Old
30 Years Old	30 Years Old	30 Years Old	30 Years Old	30 Years Old

THE CLUES

1. The oldest and youngest tortoises had matching weight and age numbers and the remaining 3 tortoises had no matching numbers.
2. The Arizona tortoise was almost eaten by a raven and is 5 years older than the Utah tortoise who was nearly eaten by a coyote.
3. The heaviest tortoise was from Nevada and had a narrow escape from a badger and the youngest tortoise was from Mexico and had a narrow escape from a fox.
4. Del, Dolly, and Denise were not native to either Mexico or Arizona and Del was not native to Utah and Del was older than Dolly but weighed 5 pounds less than Dolly. Dalia weighed 5 pounds more than Dolly.

Fat-Tailed Dunnart

THE FACTS

The fat-tailed dunnart is native to Australia and is considered one of the smallest carnivorous marsupials in the world. This marsupial only grows to a length of 60 to 90 millimeters with a fat, carrot-shaped tail adding another 45 to 70 millimeters to its length. The tail is important as this is where the dunnart stores energy in the form of fat. The weight of this marsupial is equally as small and measures between 10 to 20 grams. The fat-tailed dunnart survives on a diet of insects, beetles, larvae, worms, small lizards, snakes, frogs, and even mice. When food is scarce, the dunnart has the ability to go into a hibernation-like state called torpor where it can slow its metabolism down. In cold temperatures, the dunnart may invade a mouse's nest, not to eat it, but to snuggle with it to stay warm. There are really no natural predators of the fat-tailed dunnart and it will have a normal lifespan of about 30 months. Faye, Fred, Filo, Frank, and Finley were 5 fat-tailed dunnarts who each had a favorite food and were different lengths, weights, and ages. Based on the clues, solve the puzzle.

Faye	Fred	Filo	Frank	Finley
Insects	Insects	Insects	Insects	Insects
Beetles	Beetles	Beetles	Beetles	Beetles
Larvae	Larvae	Larvae	Larvae	Larvae
Worms	Worms	Worms	Worms	Worms
Lizards	Lizards	Lizards	Lizards	Lizards
90 mm	90 mm	90 mm	90 mm	90 mm
85 mm	85 mm	85 mm	85 mm	85 mm
80 mm	80 mm	80 mm	80 mm	80 mm
70 mm	70 mm	70 mm	70 mm	70 mm
60 mm	60 mm	60 mm	60 mm	60 mm
20 Grams	20 Grams	20 Grams	20 Grams	20 Grams
19 Grams	19 Grams	19 Grams	19 Grams	19 Grams
18 Grams	18 Grams	18 Grams	18 Grams	18 Grams
17 Grams	17 Grams	17 Grams	17 Grams	17 Grams
15 Grams	15 Grams	15 Grams	15 Grams	15 Grams
800 Days	800 Days	800 Days	800 Days	800 Days
775 Days	775 Days	775 Days	775 Days	775 Days
750 Days	750 Days	750 Days	750 Days	750 Days
725 Days	725 Days	725 Days	725 Days	725 Days
700 Days	700 Days	700 Days	700 Days	700 Days

THE CLUES

1. The longest weighed the most and loved larvae. The shortest weighed the least and loved to eat worms.
2. The 85 millimeter dunnart did not weigh 19 grams and loved to eat lizards while the 80 millimeter dunnart did not weigh 18 grams and loved to eat beetles.
3. Between the two of them, Filo and Frank had been living 1500 days but between the two of them, Fred and Finley had also been alive 1500 days.
4. Finley was not the oldest but Finley was 25 days older than Frank, Filo was older than Fred.
5. Between the two of them, Faye and Fred weighed 35 grams but Filo and Finley also had a combined weight of 35 grams, and Frank weighed 1 gram more than Finley.
6. Fred was 5 millimeters longer than Filo.

Hartebeest

THE FACTS

The hartebeest is an African grassland antelope that is still common in many African countries. The hartebeest is a good sized antelope being 59 to 96 inches long, three feet tall at the shoulder, and with a hefty weight of between 276 to 481 pounds. Both sexes have horns of between 18 to 28 inches long and this antelope has a lifespan of between 11 to 20 years in the wild. Hartebeests are social animals who live in herds of 20 to 300 individuals. Adult males, interested in romance, fight for dominance by getting on their knees and interlocking horns to determine the strongest. Their main diet is grass but it will also eat melons, roots, tubers, and legumes when available. Predators include jackals and cheetahs who prey on the very young as well as lions, hyenas, leopards, and wild dogs. Harry, Hilda, Harper, Hanne, and Harvey were 5 hartebeests who were native to 5 countries, were almost killed by different predators, and were different ages and weights. Based on the clues, solve the puzzle.

Harry	Hilda	Harper	Hanne	Harvey
Ghana	Ghana	Ghana	Ghana	Ghana
Mali	Mali	Mali	Mali	Mali
Uganda	Uganda	Uganda	Uganda	Uganda
Gambia	Gambia	Gambia	Gambia	Gambia
South Africa	South Africa	South Africa	South Africa	South Africa
Lion	Lion	Lion	Lion	Lion
Leopard	Leopard	Leopard	Leopard	Leopard
Wild Dog	Wild Dog	Wild Dog	Wild Dog	Wild Dog
Cheetah	Cheetah	Cheetah	Cheetah	Cheetah
Jackal	Jackal	Jackal	Jackal	Jackal
18 Years	18 Years	18 Years	18 Years	18 Years
16 Years	16 Years	16 Years	16 Years	16 Years
15 Years	15 Years	15 Years	15 Years	15 Years
13 Years	13 Years	13 Years	13 Years	13 Years
12 Years	12 Years	12 Years	12 Years	12 Years
450 lbs	450 lbs	450 lbs	450 lbs	450 lbs
440 lbs	440 lbs	440 lbs	440 lbs	440 lbs
400 lbs	400 lbs	400 lbs	400 lbs	400 lbs
390 lbs	390 lbs	390 lbs	390 lbs	390 lbs
350 lbs	350 lbs	350 lbs	350 lbs	350 lbs

THE CLUES

1. The oldest, youngest, and the 15 year old hartebeests were not either the heaviest or the lightest of these 5 hartebeests.
2. The Gambian hartebeest was nearly killed by a leopard and the South African hartebeest was nearly killed by a lion and neither one was either the oldest or youngest of the hartebeests.
3. Hilda was 2 years older than Harry, Hanne was 2 years older than Harvey and Harry was 1 year older than Hanne.
4. Harry was not in any danger from either a lion or a leopard. The lightest hartebeest was nearly eaten by a lion.
5. The hartebeest from Mali was nearly eaten by a jackal and weighed 10 pounds less than Harry who was never bothered by wild dogs.
6. Harper never even saw a jackal and Harper wasn't from Ghana and Hanne weighed less than Harper.

THE FACTS

The hyrax, also commonly called a "dassie" is a small chubby herbivorous mammal native to virtually every country in sub-Saharan Africa. The hyrax reaches lengths of 12 to 28 inches and weighs between 4 and 11 pounds. The hyrax is the closest living relative of the elephant despite the wide difference in size. Shared characteristics between the elephant and the hyrax include excellent hearing, good memories, high intelligence, incisor teeth which grow into tusks, and both males have hidden scrotums. Hyraxes live in small family groups led by a dominant male and subsist on a diet of grass, leaves, fruit, Insects, lizards, and eggs. The hyrax has a lifespan of 12 years or so. Hayley, Hart, Hassie, Hank, and Hazel were 5 hyrax native to 5 countries and were different lengths, weights, and ages. Based on the clues, solve the puzzle.

Hayley	Hart	Hassie	Hank	Hazel
Benin	Benin	Benin	Benin	Benin
Botswana	Botswana	Botswana	Botswana	Botswana
Kenya	Kenya	Kenya	Kenya	Kenya
Rwanda	Rwanda	Rwanda	Rwanda	Rwanda
South Africa	South Africa	South Africa	South Africa	South Africa
28 in	28 in	28 in	28 in	28 in
27 in	27 in	27 in	27 in	27 in
26 in	26 in	26 in	26 in	26 in
24 in	24 in	24 in	24 in	24 in
22 in	22 in	22 in	22 in	22 in
11 lbs	11 lbs	11 lbs	11 lbs	11 lbs
10 lbs	10 lbs	10 lbs	10 lbs	10 lbs
9 lbs	9 lbs	9 lbs	9 lbs	9 lbs
8 lbs	8 lbs	8 lbs	8 lbs	8 lbs
7 lbs	7 lbs	7 lbs	7 lbs	7 lbs
11 Years	11 Years	11 Years	11 Years	11 Years
10 Years	10 Years	10 Years	10 Years	10 Years
9 Years	9 Years	9 Years	9 Years	9 Years
8 Years	8 Years	8 Years	8 Years	8 Years
7 Years	7 Years	7 Years	7 Years	7 Years

THE CLUES

1. Three of the hyraxes have exactly matching weight and age numbers which means the remaining two do not have numbers that match.
2. The heaviest hyrax was from Rwanda, was 26 inches, and was the youngest hyrax listed here.
3. The oldest hyrax was from Botswana, was 27 inches, and weighed the least of the hyraxes listed here.
4. Hayley weighed 1 pound more than Hart, Hart weighed 1 pound more than Hassie, Hassie weighed 1 pound more than Hazel.
5. Hayley wasn't the youngest hyrax, the longest hyrax was from South Africa, and Hassie was 2 inches longer than Hank.
6. The shortest hyrax was from Benin and Hart was not from Kenya.

Marmot

THE FACTS

There are 14 species of marmot in the world but they are all just giant fat ground squirrels. Their fat does more than make them appear cuddly as they need the stored energy to survive their nine months of hibernation they spend deep in their sealed burrows. Although they are social animals, it is family members only when it comes to hibernating companions. Adult marmots reach a length of between 11 to 24 inches and weigh between 6 to 15 pounds or so. Marmots prefer life at higher elevations and can be found in European mountain ranges such as the Alps, Apennines, and Pyrenees as well as North American mountains such as the Rockies or Sierra Nevada Mountains. Marmots survive on a diet of grass, berries, lichens, moss, roots, and flowers as well as grubs, grasshoppers, Insects, worms, and snails when available. Marmots have a normal lifespan of at least 10 years. Maria, Marty, Miles, Morton, and Mabel were 5 marmots living in 5 different mountain ranges who were different lengths and weights and each had a different favorite food. Based on the clues, solve the puzzle.

Maria	Marty	Miles	Morton	Mabel
Alps	Alps	Alps	Alps	Alps
Apennines	Apennines	Apennines	Apennines	Apennines
Pyrenees	Pyrenees	Pyrenees	Pyrenees	Pyrenees
Rockies	Rockies	Rockies	Rockies	Rockies
Sierra Nevada	Sierra Nevada	Sierra Nevada	Sierra Nevada	Sierra Nevada
24 in	24 in	24 in	24 in	24 in
22 in	22 in	22 in	22 in	22 in
20 in	20 in	20 in	20 in	20 in
15 in	15 in	15 in	15 in	15 in
14 in	14 in	14 in	14 in	14 in
15 lbs	15 lbs	15 lbs	15 lbs	15 lbs
14 lbs	14 lbs	14 lbs	14 lbs	14 lbs
13 lbs	13 lbs	13 lbs	13 lbs	13 lbs
12 lbs	12 lbs	12 lbs	12 lbs	12 lbs
10 lbs	10 lbs	10 lbs	10 lbs	10 lbs
Grass	Grass	Grass	Grass	Grass
Moss	Moss	Moss	Moss	Moss
Lichens	Lichens	Lichens	Lichens	Lichens
Grubs	Grubs	Grubs	Grubs	Grubs
Snails	Snails	Snails	Snails	Snails

THE CLUES

1. The two marmots living in the Rockies and Sierra Nevada had length numbers exactly twice as large as their weight numbers.
2. The two marmots living in the Pyrenees and Apennines had length and weight numbers that match exactly.
3. Mabel was 2 inches longer than Maria but Marty was 2 inches longer than Mabel.
4. The longest marmot's favorite food did not include moss or grubs and the 2 heaviest marmots thought grass and lichens were their favorite foods.
5. The Sierra Nevada marmot loved grubs, the heaviest marmot lived in the Pyrenees and did not like grass.
6. Morton was shorter than Miles.

THE FACTS

The oven bird is a relatively small migratory songbird who breeds during the summer in eastern North America and migrates south in the winter. The oven bird gets its common name from the nests it constructs on the ground which look like early outdoor ovens complete with a side entrance. Adult oven birds are 11 to 15 centimeters long with wingspans of between 19 to 26 centimeters across. Oven birds are territorial both in their summer and winter homes. An interesting trait of the oven bird is the fact that males and females split their broods at about the age of 30 days and raise their chicks separately. Oven birds are used to migrating long distances but some oven birds have actually been able to cross the Atlantic Ocean which is an astounding feat of endurance for any land dwelling bird. Of the six oven birds known to have accomplished this feat, three were found dead of exhaustion which is an indication of how difficult this journey is. The oven bird has a lifespan of about 12 years. Ollie, Ovid, Otto, Ona, and Ophelia were 5 oven birds born in 5 different places, had different wingspans, migrated different distances, and were different ages. Based on the clues, solve the puzzle.

Ollie	Ovid	Otto	Ona	Ophelia
New York	New York	New York	New York	New York
Vermont	Vermont	Vermont	Vermont	Vermont
Maine	Maine	Maine	Maine	Maine
Quebec	Quebec	Quebec	Quebec	Quebec
Ontario	Ontario	Ontario	Ontario	Ontario
26 cm	26 cm	26 cm	26 cm	26 cm
25 cm	25 cm	25 cm	25 cm	25 cm
24 cm	24 cm	24 cm	24 cm	24 cm
23 cm	23 cm	23 cm	23 cm	23 cm
21 cm	21 cm	21 cm	21 cm	21 cm
1500 Miles	1500 Miles	1500 Miles	1500 Miles	1500 Miles
1450 Miles	1450 Miles	1450 Miles	1450 Miles	1450 Miles
1425 Miles	1425 Miles	1425 Miles	1425 Miles	1425 Miles
1400 Miles	1400 Miles	1400 Miles	1400 Miles	1400 Miles
1375 Miles	1375 Miles	1375 Miles	1375 Miles	1375 Miles
12 Years	12 Years	12 Years	12 Years	12 Years
11 Years	11 Years	11 Years	11 Years	11 Years
10 Years	10 Years	10 Years	10 Years	10 Years
9 Years	9 Years	9 Years	9 Years	9 Years
8 Years	8 Years	8 Years	8 Years	8 Years

THE CLUES

1. The oven bird born in Ontario had the widest wingspan, migrated the longest distance, and was the oldest bird.
2. The oven bird born in Quebec had the smallest wingspan, migrated the shortest distance, and was the youngest bird.
3. Ona wasn't born in Maine and Ona migrated 25 miles farther than Otto but Otto migrated 25 miles farther than Ophelia who wasn't born in Quebec or Maine.
4. Ona was 1 year younger than the oven bird born in Vermont with the 23 centimeter wingspan.
5. Ovid was 1 year younger than the Maine-born oven bird.
6. Otto's wingspan was smaller than Ona's wingspan.

THE FACTS

The peccary, also known as a javelina or skunk pig, is a medium-sized mammal often confused with feral pigs. There is some resemblance but the peccary is entirely native to the Americas and a different family than the Afro-Eurasian pig either domesticated or wild. Peccaries may be found in states such as Arizona and countries such as Mexico, Costa Rica, Paraguay, Bolivia, Argentina, and Brazil. Peccaries achieve an adult length of between 90 to 130 centimeters and weights of between 44 to 88 pounds. Peccaries are social animals and choose to live in herds of up to 100 individuals. Female peccaries leave the herd to give birth because if she didn't, members of the herd would gobble down her newborn. Peccaries are very near-sighted and depend on their strong scent glands to identify each other. Peccaries can be very aggressive and herds of them have been known to attack and kill humans. Peccaries have lifespans of up to 24 years. Pete, Pilar, Polly, Paul, and Paddy were 5 peccaries who lived in different sized herds and were different ages. Based on the clues, solve the puzzle.

Pete	Pilar	Polly	Paul	Paddy
Arizona	Arizona	Arizona	Arizona	Arizona
Mexico	Mexico	Mexico	Mexico	Mexico
Argentina	Argentina	Argentina	Argentina	Argentina
Brazil	Brazil	Brazil	Brazil	Brazil
Bolivia	Bolivia	Bolivia	Bolivia	Bolivia
85 lbs	85 lbs	85 lbs	85 lbs	85 lbs
82 lbs	82 lbs	82 lbs	82 lbs	82 lbs
79 lbs	79 lbs	79 lbs	79 lbs	79 lbs
76 lbs	76 lbs	76 lbs	76 lbs	76 lbs
75 lbs	75 lbs	75 lbs	75 lbs	75 lbs
100 Herd	100 Herd	100 Herd	100 Herd	100 Herd
90 Herd	90 Herd	90 Herd	90 Herd	90 Herd
85 Herd	85 Herd	85 Herd	85 Herd	85 Herd
75 Herd	75 Herd	75 Herd	75 Herd	75 Herd
70 Herd	70 Herd	70 Herd	70 Herd	70 Herd
20 Years	20 Years	20 Years	20 Years	20 Years
18 Years	18 Years	18 Years	18 Years	18 Years
15 Years	15 Years	15 Years	15 Years	15 Years
13 Years	13 Years	13 Years	13 Years	13 Years
11 Years	11 Years	11 Years	11 Years	11 Years

THE CLUES

1. The oldest peccary lived in the largest herd, the 2nd oldest lived in the 2nd largest herd, the 3rd oldest lived in the 3rd largest herd, and the same pattern is true for the 4th and 5th oldest peccaries.
2. The weight and herd size number exactly match for the peccaries from Arizona and Bolivia.
3. Pete, Pilar, and Polly were the 3 heaviest peccaries and none of these 3 were from either Brazil or Bolivia.
4. Pete wasn't from Mexico and Pete weighed 3 pounds more than Pilar and Pilar weighed 3 pounds more than Paddy who wasn't from Bolivia.
5. Paddy was 2 years older than the peccary from Mexico and Polly was not from Argentina.

Tiger Quoll

THE FACTS

There are six species of quolls all native to Australia, New Guinea, and Tasmania. Quolls are carnivorous marsupials who make their living by hunting and killing other animals. The tiger quoll is the largest of the six species with a length of up to 30 inches with a bushy tail adding another 14 inches and a weight ranging from 8 to 15 pounds. Quolls are nocturnal hunters and spend their days sleeping in hollow logs or rock crevices. Quolls prefer the solitary life except during breeding season and when emptying their bowels. Several quolls in an area will designate one spot as a communal latrine and all quolls in an area will meet and defecate in the same spot. Tiger quolls subsist on a diet of brushtail possums, rabbits, hares, bandicoots, birds, lizards, frogs, and will even resort to eating carrion. The normal lifespan of a tiger quoll is about 60 months. Troy, Talya, Timmy, Tara, and Tippi were 5 tiger quolls who kept a record of their catches in one recent month. Based on the clues, solve the puzzle.

Troy	Talya	Timmy	Tara	Tippi
12 Possums	12 Possums	12 Possums	12 Possums	12 Possums
10 Possums	10 Possums	10 Possums	10 Possums	10 Possums
8 Possums	8 Possums	8 Possums	8 Possums	8 Possums
6 Possums	6 Possums	6 Possums	6 Possums	6 Possums
4 Possums	4 Possums	4 Possums	4 Possums	4 Possums
12 Rabbits	12 Rabbits	12 Rabbits	12 Rabbits	12 Rabbits
10 Rabbits	10 Rabbits	10 Rabbits	10 Rabbits	10 Rabbits
8 Rabbits	8 Rabbits	8 Rabbits	8 Rabbits	8 Rabbits
6 Rabbits	6 Rabbits	6 Rabbits	6 Rabbits	6 Rabbits
4 Rabbits	4 Rabbits	4 Rabbits	4 Rabbits	4 Rabbits
6 Birds	6 Birds	6 Birds	6 Birds	6 Birds
5 Birds	5 Birds	5 Birds	5 Birds	5 Birds
4 Birds	4 Birds	4 Birds	4 Birds	4 Birds
3 Birds	3 Birds	3 Birds	3 Birds	3 Birds
2 Birds	2 Birds	2 Birds	2 Birds	2 Birds
6 Lizards	6 Lizards	6 Lizards	6 Lizards	6 Lizards
5 Lizards	5 Lizards	5 Lizards	5 Lizards	5 Lizards
4 Lizards	4 Lizards	4 Lizards	4 Lizards	4 Lizards
3 Lizards	3 Lizards	3 Lizards	3 Lizards	3 Lizards
2 Lizards	2 Lizards	2 Lizards	2 Lizards	2 Lizards

THE CLUES

1. Except for Timmy, each of the quolls ate the most of 1 food group, the 2nd most of another food group, the 3rd most of another food group, and the 5th most of yet another food group.
2. Troy ate 2 more possums than Talya, Tara ate 2 more rabbits than Tippi and Tippi ate 1 more bird than Tara.
3. Talya ate 1 more bird than Timmy and Tippi ate 2 more rabbits than Troy.
4. Tara ate more lizards than Timmy.

THE FACTS

The kiskadee is a rather large songbird common throughout South and Central America up through Mexico and into the southern portion of Texas. The kiskadee is easily recognizable by its bright yellow-belly, feathers, and its distinctive call which sounds like it is repeating the word "kiskadee" over and over. The bird is about a foot long with a weight of about 2 ½ ounces. Kiskadees mate for life and together defend their territory and participate together in feeding and protecting their young. Kiskadees are opportunistic feeders and will eat beetles, wasps, moths, grasshoppers, bees, mice, frogs, fish, tadpoles, baby birds, berries, seeds, and lizards. Karen, Kerwin, Kerry, Kate, and Kelly were 5 kiskadees who were watched one day and their food consumption monitored. They ate different numbers of 5 different food items. Based on the clues, solve the puzzle.

Karen	Kerwin	Kerry	Kate	Kelly
7 Bees	7 Bees	7 Bees	7 Bees	7 Bees
6 Bees	6 Bees	6 Bees	6 Bees	6 Bees
4 Bees	4 Bees	4 Bees	4 Bees	4 Bees
3 Bees	3 Bees	3 Bees	3 Bees	3 Bees
1 Bee	1 Bee	1 Bee	1 Bee	1 Bee
5 Wasps	5 Wasps	5 Wasps	5 Wasps	5 Wasps
4 Wasps	4 Wasps	4 Wasps	4 Wasps	4 Wasps
3 Wasps	3 Wasps	3 Wasps	3 Wasps	3 Wasps
2 Wasps	2 Wasps	2 Wasps	2 Wasps	2 Wasps
1 Wasp	1 Wasp	1 Wasp	1 Wasp	1 Wasp
8 Moths	8 Moths	8 Moths	8 Moths	8 Moths
6 Moths	6 Moths	6 Moths	6 Moths	6 Moths
4 Moths	4 Moths	4 Moths	4 Moths	4 Moths
3 Moths	3 Moths	3 Moths	3 Moths	3 Moths
2 Moths	2 Moths	2 Moths	2 Moths	2 Moths
9 Beetles	9 Beetles	9 Beetles	9 Beetles	9 Beetles
7 Beetles	7 Beetles	7 Beetles	7 Beetles	7 Beetles
5 Beetles	5 Beetles	5 Beetles	5 Beetles	5 Beetles
4 Beetles	4 Beetles	4 Beetles	4 Beetles	4 Beetles
3 Beetles	3 Beetles	3 Beetles	3 Beetles	3 Beetles
5 Grasshoppers	5 Grasshoppers	5 Grasshoppers	5 Grasshoppers	5 Grasshoppers
4 Grasshoppers	4 Grasshoppers	4 Grasshoppers	4 Grasshoppers	4 Grasshoppers
3 Grasshoppers	3 Grasshoppers	3 Grasshoppers	3 Grasshoppers	3 Grasshoppers
2 Grasshoppers	2 Grasshoppers	2 Grasshoppers	2 Grasshoppers	2 Grasshoppers
1 Grasshopper	1 Grasshopper	1 Grasshopper	1 Grasshopper	1 Grasshopper

THE CLUES

1. One kiskadee ate the most of 3 food items and ate the fewest of 2 food items and another kiskadee ate the most of 2 food items and the fewest of 3 food items.
2. One kiskadee ate the 2nd largest number of all 5 food items and another kiskadee ate the 3rd largest number of three different food items and that kiskadee had to eat the 4th largest number of 2 items.
3. Kerwin ate 1 more bee than Kelly and while Kate didn't eat the most bees, Kate ate 1 more bee than Karen.
4. Kate ate 1 more wasp than Karen and Kerry ate fewer wasps than Karen.
5. Kerry ate more grasshoppers than Kate, Kate ate more moths than Kerwin, and Kerry ate more beetles than Karen.

THE FACTS

Native to the Atlantic Ocean and the Mediterranean Sea, the Bluefin tuna is not the tuna you will find in your tuna salad sandwiches. The Bluefin tuna is highly prized and priced as the main ingredient in sushi and sashimi. The Bluefin tuna has a rhomboidal shaped body, and will usually be 6 to 8 feet long. They routinely weigh from 490 to 550 pounds when fully mature. The Bluefin tuna is warm-blooded and has the ability to "thermos regulate" itself to survive and thrive in the chilly waters of the Atlantic Ocean. Bluefin tuna prey includes sardines, herring, mackerel, squid, and shrimp. Bluefin tuna can swim at up to an amazing 40 mph if necessary. The Bluefin tuna has a normal lifespan of about 50 years. Byron, Bess, Bev, Blake, and Betty were 5 Bluefin tuna who decided to have a contest to see who could eat the most of 5 different Bluefin tuna food items. Based on the clues, solve the puzzle.

Byron	Bess	Bev	Blake	Betty
50 Sardines	50 Sardines	50 Sardines	50 Sardines	50 Sardines
48 Sardines	48 Sardines	48 Sardines	48 Sardines	48 Sardines
47 Sardines	47 Sardines	47 Sardines	47 Sardines	47 Sardines
46 Sardines	46 Sardines	46 Sardines	46 Sardines	46 Sardines
44 Sardines	44 Sardines	44 Sardines	44 Sardines	44 Sardines
25 Herring	25 Herring	25 Herring	25 Herring	25 Herring
24 Herring	24 Herring	24 Herring	24 Herring	24 Herring
22 Herring	22 Herring	22 Herring	22 Herring	22 Herring
20 Herring	20 Herring	20 Herring	20 Herring	20 Herring
18 Herring	18 Herring	18 Herring	18 Herring	18 Herring
15 Mackerel	15 Mackerel	15 Mackerel	15 Mackerel	15 Mackerel
14 Mackerel	14 Mackerel	14 Mackerel	14 Mackerel	14 Mackerel
13 Mackerel	13 Mackerel	13 Mackerel	13 Mackerel	13 Mackerel
12 Mackerel	12 Mackerel	12 Mackerel	12 Mackerel	12 Mackerel
10 Mackerel	10 Mackerel	10 Mackerel	10 Mackerel	10 Mackerel
100 Squid	100 Squid	100 Squid	100 Squid	100 Squid
96 Squid	96 Squid	96 Squid	96 Squid	96 Squid
95 Squid	95 Squid	95 Squid	95 Squid	95 Squid
92 Squid	92 Squid	92 Squid	92 Squid	92 Squid
88 Squid	88 Squid	88 Squid	88 Squid	88 Squid
35 Shrimp	35 Shrimp	35 Shrimp	35 Shrimp	35 Shrimp
30 Shrimp	30 Shrimp	30 Shrimp	30 Shrimp	30 Shrimp
25 Shrimp	25 Shrimp	25 Shrimp	25 Shrimp	25 Shrimp
20 Shrimp	20 Shrimp	20 Shrimp	20 Shrimp	20 Shrimp
15 Shrimp	15 Shrimp	15 Shrimp	15 Shrimp	15 Shrimp

THE CLUES

1. By an amazing coincidence, each bluefin tuna ate the most of 1 food item, the 2nd most of 1 food item, the 3rd most of 1 food item, the 4th most of 1 food item, and the least of 1 food item.
2. Bess ate 2 more sardines than Blake, Betty ate 2 more sardines than Byron, and Blake ate more sardines than Bev.
3. Bess ate 1 more mackerel than Byron, Byron ate 1 more mackerel than Bev.
4. Betty ate 4 more squid than Byron and Bess ate 4 more squid than Bev.
5. Byron did not eat the most herring.

1. Tarsier

Tammy	Tom	Tillie	Terry	Tess
Luzon	Sumatra	Borneo	Solanesi	Sarawak
63 cm	70 cm	68 cm	65 cm	67 cm
Birds	Insects	Snakes	Lizards	Bats
16 Years	17 Years	12 Years	14 Years	18 Years

2. Wild Turkey

Tara	Toots	Trina	Taylor	Toni
44 in	42 in	49 in	48 in	46 in
23 lbs	24 lbs	18 lbs	20 lbs	22 lbs
11 Eggs	10 Eggs	14 Eggs	13 Eggs	12 Eggs
Fox	Skunk	Raccoon	Coyote	Groundhog

3. Canada Goose

Giles	Grace	Gavin	Gina	Gary
Russia	China	Japan	Germany	France
13 lbs	11 lbs	12 lbs	16 lbs	15 lbs
73 in wing	66 in wing	68 in wing	71 in wing	70 in wing
13 Years	20 Years	18 Years	16 Years	15 Years

4. House Sparrow

Sidney	Sylvia	Sheba	Shep	Shari
Canada	China	France	Spain	Japan
14 cm	18 cm	17 cm	16 cm	15 cm
18 Years	14 Years	15 Years	16 Years	17 Years
Wheat	Cherries	Grapes	Oats	Insects

5. Binturong

Ben	Binnie	Belle	Brad	Barry
in.onesia	India	Thialand	Vietnam	Laos
53 in	58 in	60 in	55 in	50 in
65 lbs	70 lbs	65 lbs	55 lbs	50 lbs
15 Years	16 Years	15 Years	18 Years	20 Years

6. Northern Caiman Lizard

Carrie	Cathy	Carl	Conrad	Cindi
Peru	Ecuador	Guyana	Brazil	Columbia
Insects	Snails	Rodents	Crawfish	Clams
48 in	42 in	47 in	44 in	46 in
16 Years	18 Years	14 Years	20 Years	10 Years

7. Clown Fish

Cora	Callie	Candy	Cyndy	Chandra
White	Blue	Nurse	Tiger	Mako
14 cm	15 cm	17 cm	18 cm	16 cm
700 Eggs	600 Eggs	1200 Eggs	1400 Eggs	1300 Eggs
43 Months	41 Months	45 Months	50 Months	48 Months

8. Donkey

Dana	Dave	Dina	Don	Danny
Ethiopia	Mexico	Egypt	Chin	Pakistan
60 in tall	50 in tall	53 in tall	55 in tall	58 in tall
800 lbs	700 lbs	725 lbs	775 lbs	750 lbs
30 Years	25 Years	20 Years	15 Years	10 Years

9. Gar

Gayle	Gordy	Gene	Gigi	Gwen
Frog	Crawfish	Perch	Bluegill	Herring
34 in	36 in	32 in	29 in	31 in
46 lbs	47 lbs	43 lbs	50 lbs	49 lbs
17 Years	18 Years	16 Years	20 Years	19 Years

10. Hercules Beetle

Hester	Helga	Heidi	Helen	Hilda
Columbia	Ecuador	Brazil	Peru	Mexico
18 cm	20 cm	19 cm	16 cm	17 cm
265 oz	260 oz	270 oz	268 oz	263 oz
90 Eggs	80 Eggs	100 Eggs	95 Eggs	85 Eggs

11. Iriomote Cat

Inez	Igor	Iggy	Ilsa	Irene
56 cm	58 cm	60 cm	54 cm	59 cm
166 oz	164 oz	168 oz	176 oz	172 oz
Bats	Frogs	Birds	Snakes	Rats
5 Years	4 Years	8 Years	6 Years	7 Years

12. Jackal

Jack	Jill	Josey	Jenny	Jane
Rwanda	Kenya	Congo	India	Egypt
38 in	39 in	42 in	41 in	40 in
31 lbs	32 lbs	35 lbs	34 lbs	33 lbs
10 Years	9 Years	6 Years	7 Years	8 Years

13. Leopard Seal

Larry	Lucy	Linda	Les	Lulu
2 King	6 King	8 King	4 King	10 King
1 Adelie	3 Adelie	4 Adelie	2 Adelie	5 Adelie
2 Gentoo	6 Gentoo	4 Gentoo	8 Gentoo	10 Gentoo
1 Emperor	3 Emperor	2 Emperor	4 Emperor	5 Emperor

14. Sea Otter

Ozzie	Ollie	Oppie	Olive	Oona
Alaska	Aleutians	British Columbia	Washington	Russia
Snails	Mussels	Sea Urchins	Abalone	Clams
85 lbs	90 lbs	70 lbs	80 lbs	75 lbs
16 Years	17 Years	18 Years	20 Years	14 Years

15. King Vulture

Vicky	Vera	Val	Viola	Vlad
Deer	Horse	Pig	Goat	Cow
Mexico	Peru	Panama	Brazil	Columbia
72 in wing	70 in wing	67 in wing	69 in wing	68 in wing
23 Years	25 Years	20 Years	17 Years	14 Years

16. Potgut

Polly	Paula	Penny	Pearl	Patty
34 cm	38 cm	36 cm	32 cm	35 cm
2 young	6 young	5 young	4 young	3 young
6 Years Old	5 Years Old	4 Years Old	3 Years Old	2 Years Old
Hawk	Weasel	Badger	Wolf	Coyote

17. Australian Water Dragon

Walt	Willa	Wallis	Winnie	Westy
12 Years old	6 Years old	16 Years old	8 Years old	14 Years old
12 Ants	6 Ants	8 Ants	16 Ants	14 Ants
12 Crickets	14 Crickets	8 Crickets	16 Crickets	6 Crickets
12 Beetles	14 Beetles	16 Beetles	8 Beetles	6 Beetles

18. Loris

Livia	Lane	Layla	Lorna	Louis
4 Mice	5 Mice	3 Mice	1 Mice	2 Mice
40 Insects	35 Insects	45 Insects	50 Insects	48 Insects
25 Leaves	24 Leaves	20 Leaves	15 Leaves	10 Leaves
2 Eggs	4 Eggs	6 Eggs	8 Eggs	10 Eggs

19. Potto

Paul	Patrick	Paris	Pete	Pella
Uganda	Senegal	Guinea	Kenya	Congo
38 cm	39 cm	36 cm	34 cm	32 cm
48 oz	45 oz	50 oz	53 oz	56 oz
18 Years	20 Years	17 Years	16 Years	14 Years

20. Frogfish

Frank	Flo	Filene	Farrah	Foster
Indian	Pacific	Java Sea	Red Sea	Atlantic
Yellow	Brown	Purple	Black	Green
14 in	13 in	10 in	12 in	15 in
5 Years	7 Years	10 Years	9 Years	4 Years

21. Stingray

Sam	Sara	Spike	Sylvia	Shari
20 Years Old	16 Years Old	18 Years Old	15 Years Old	12 Years Old
20 Clams	16 Clams	18 Clams	13 Clams	12 Clams
11 Oysters	13 Oysters	16 Oysters	10 Oysters	12 Oysters
11 Snails	13 Snails	9 Snails	10 Snails	12 Snails

22. Parrotfish

Petra	Pete	Pilar	Patty	Paul
Peurto Rico	Trindad	Bermuda	Cuba	Aruba
18 ft	20 ft	17 ft	16 ft	15 ft
20 in long	15 in long	17 in long	16 in long	18 in long
3 Years	4 Years	7 Years	6 Years	5 Years

23. Iberian Lynx

Iris	Irene	in.o	Ivan	Ilsa
40 in	43 in	42 in	41 in	39 in
40 lbs	43 lbs	42 lbs	41 lbs	39 lbs
10 Rabbits	6 Rabbits	9 Rabbits	4 Rabbits	8 Rabbits
10 Years	6 Years	9 Years	4 Years	8 Years

24. Tailless Tenrec

Tess	Tina	Tom	Troy	Tanya
Mauritius	Comoros	Madagascar	Seychelles	Reunion
12 in	16 in	10 in	15 in	14 in
80 oz	96 oz	76 oz	88 oz	92 oz
6 Years old	8 Years old	10 Years old	9 Years old	7 Years old

25. Boa Constrictor

Carl	Connie	Cora	Cathy	Craig
Panama	Brazil	Mexico	Venezuela	Bolivia
13 ft	12 ft	14 ft	10 ft	9 ft
Monkey	Pig	Rat	Lizard	Bat
26 Years Old	24 Years Old	28 Years Old	20 Years Old	18 Years Old

26. Weasel

Willy	Wanda	Wayne	Walt	Wendy
30 months	28 months	24 months	20 months	16 months
Fox	Hawk	Snake	Coyote	Owl
10 Rats	6 Rats	7 Rats	8 Rats	9 Rats
6 Mice	10 Mice	9 Mice	8 Mice	7 Mice

27. Monkfish

Morrie	Manny	Marie	Mame	Mona
10 Years Old	15 Years Old	14 Years Old	12 Years Old	11 Years Old
53 in	60 in	55 in	50 in	58 in
20 Herring	30 Herring	28 Herring	25 Herring	29 Herring
20 Sardines	15 Sardines	18 Sardines	25 Sardines	10 Sardines

28. Climbing Perch

Cecil	Carl	Chandra	Cindy	Cassie
Lake	Puddle	River	Stream	Pond
23 cm	21 cm	25 cm	24 cm	22 cm
10,000 ft	9,500 ft	9,300 ft	9,100 ft	8,900 ft
6 Days	8 Days	4 Days	5 Days	7 Days

29. Swan

Sally	Sarah	Sheena	Sophie	Sybil
54 in	56 in	60 in	58 in	57 in
33 lbs	32 lbs	30 lbs	29 lbs	31 lbs
10 Years Old	12 Years Old	13 Years Old	15 Years Old	9 Years Old
5 Eggs	6 Eggs	4 Eggs	7 Eggs	8 Eggs

30. Anaconda

Arnie	Alex	April	Annie	Art
Brazil	Bolivia	Peru	Ecuador	Columbia
31 ft	25 ft	32 ft	29 ft	27 ft
490 lbs	500 lbs	400 lbs	460 lbs	450 lbs
Monkey	Deer	Tapir	Caiman	Cabybara

31. Dall Sheep

Dave	Deedee	Dian	Dylan	Danny
8,500 ft	10,000 ft	9,500 ft	8,000 ft	9,000 ft
Eagle	Wolf	Coyote	Grizzly	Lynx
230 lbs	180 lbs	200 lbs	250 lbs	210 lbs
11 Years Old	5 Years Old	12 Years Old	9 Years Old	7 Years Old

32. Flamingo

Fanny	Frank	Flo	Ferris	Finley
43 in	40 in	45 in	35 in	38 in
75 oz	80 oz	90 oz	70 oz	86 oz
32 mph	33 mph	31 mph	35 mph	34 mph
16 Years	17 Years	15 Years	20 Years	18 Years

33. Skipjack Tuna

Skippy	Shari	Sheila	Sonny	Sam
32 in	38 in	37 in	35 in	34 in
28 lbs	22 lbs	24 lbs	26 lbs	27 lbs
Rosie	Tom	Beth	Randy	Ryan
Sardine	Anchovy	Squid	Herring	Perch

34. Aardwolf

Ava	Amy	Arthur	Albert	Alice
250,000	245,000	240,000	230,000	225,000
27 in long	31 in long	28 in long	25 in long	30 in long
29 lbs	26 lbs	28 lbs	25 lbs	30 lbs
14 Years	13 Years	12 Years	10 Years	8 Years

35. Avocet

Andy	Avis	Astrid	Armin	Astor
Florida	Mexico	Alberta	Manitoba	Texas
13 Years	10 Years	15 Years	14 Years	12 Years
26 in	25 in	30 in	27 in	28 in
13 oz	10 oz	15 oz	12 oz	14 oz

36. Arrow Worm

Wendy	Wilma	Westy	Willy	Wayne
75 mm	80 mm	100 mm	95 mm	85 mm
40 Organisms	38 Organisms	28 Organisms	35 Organisms	33 Organisms
10 months old	16 months old	24 months old	22 months old	18 months old
Larvae	Arrow Worms	Chordates	Copepods	Krill

37. Australian Brush Turkey

Beth	Beryl	Birdie	Brin	Bonnie
17 Years old	15 Years old	20 Years old	18 Years old	16 Years old
17 Eggs	15 Eggs	20 Eggs	18 Eggs	16 Eggs
12 Males	13 Males	11 Males	10 Males	9 Males
5 Females	2 Females	9 Females	8 Females	7 Females

38. Pampas Fox

Paul	Pete	Peri	Pela	Penn
75 Insects	100 Insects	90 Insects	80 Insects	85 Insects
10 Mice	4 Mice	9 Mice	5 Mice	7 Mice
3 Frogs	4 Frogs	6 Frogs	7 Frogs	2 Frogs
11 Snails	11 Snails	13 Snails	9 Snails	12 Snails

39. Desert Tortoise

Del	Dolly	Denise	Donald	Dalia
California	Utah	Nevada	Mexico	Arizona
Gila Monster	Coyote	Badger	Fox	Raven
35 lbs	40 lbs	50 lbs	30 lbs	45 lbs
45 Years Old	35 Years Old	50 Years Old	30 Years Old	40 Years Old

40. Fat-Tailed Dunnart

Faye	Fred	Filo	Frank	Finley
Worms	Larvae	Lizards	Beetles	Insects
60 mm	90 mm	85 mm	80 mm	70 mm
15 grams	20 grams	17 grams	19 grams	18 grams
750 days	775 days	800 days	700 days	725 days

41. Hartebeest

Harry	Hilda	Harper	Hanne	Harvey
Ghana	Mali	Uganda	Gambia	South Africa
Cheetah	Jackal	Wild Dog	Leopard	Lion
16 Years	18 Years	12 Years	15 Years	13 Years
450 lbs	440 lbs	400 lbs	390 lbs	350 lbs

42. Hyrax

Hayley	Hart	Hassie	Hank	Hazel
Kenya	Benin	South Africa	Rwanda	Botswana
24 in	22 in	28 in	26 in	27 in
10 lbs	9 lbs	8 lbs	11 lbs	7 lbs
10 Years	9 Years	8 Years	7 Years	11 Years

43. Marmot

Maria	Marty	Miles	Morton	Mabel
Sierra Nevada	Rockies	Pyrenees	Apennines	Alps
20 in	24 in	15 in	14 in	22 in
10 lbs	12 lbs	15 lbs	14 lbs	13 lbs
Grubs	Snails	Lichens	Grass	Moss

44. Oven Bird

Ollie	Ovid	Otto	Ona	Ophelia
Ontario	Quebec	Maine	New York	Vermont
26 cm	21 cm	24 cm	25 cm	23 cm
1500 Miles	1375 Miles	1425 Miles	1450 Miles	1400 Miles
12 Years	8 Years	9 Years	10 Years	11 Years

45. Peccary

Pete	Pilar	Polly	Paul	Paddy
Argentina	Mexico	Arizona	Bolivia	Brazil
82 lbs	79 lbs	85 lbs	75 lbs	76 lbs
70 Herd	90 Herd	85 Herd	75 Herd	100 Herd
11 Years	18 Years	15 Years	13 Years	20 Years

46. Tiger Quoll

Troy	Tayla	Timmy	Tara	Tippi
12 Possums	10 Possums	6 Possums	4 Possums	8 Possums
8 Rabbits	4 Rabbits	6 Rabbits	12 Rabbits	10 Rabbits
2 Birds	4 Birds	3 Birds	5 Birds	6 Birds
5 Lizards	6 Lizards	3 Lizards	4 Lizards	2 Lizards

47. Kiskadee

Karen	Kerwin	Kerry	Kate	Kelly
3 Bees	7 Bees	1 Bees	4 Bees	6 Bees
2 Wasps	5 Wasps	1 Wasps	3 Wasps	4 Wasps
4 Moths	2 Moths	8 Moths	3 Moths	6 Moths
5 Beetles	3 Beetles	9 Beetles	4 Beetles	7 Beetles
3 Grasshoppers	1 Grasshoppers	5 Grasshoppers	2 Grasshoppers	4 Grasshoppers

48. Atlantic Bluefin Tuna

Byron	Bess	Bev	Blake	Betty
44 Sardines	50 Sardines	47 Sardines	48 Sardines	46 Sardines
20 Herrings	22 Herrings	25 Herrings	18 Herrings	24 Herrings
13 Mackerel	14 Mackerel	12 Mackerel	15 Mackerel	10 Mackerel
96 Squid	92 Squid	88 Squid	95 Squid	100 Squid
35 Shrimp	15 Shrimp	30 Shrimp	20 Shrimp	25 Shrimp